THE ROMAN CATHOLIC TRADITION:

CHRISTIAN LIFESTYLE

AND BEHAVIOUR

Joanne Cleave

Heinemann

Mark, Jenn and Mike. I wrote this book for you. With Love.

Heinemann Educational Publishers
Halley Court, Jordan Hill, Oxford, OX2 8EJ
a division of Reed Educational and Professional
Publishing Ltd

OXFORD MELBOURNE AUCKLAND
JOHANNESBURG BLANTYRE GABORONE
IBADAN PORTSMOUTH (NH) USA CHICAGO

Heinemann is a registered trademark of Reed
Educational and Professional Publishing Ltd

Text © Joanne Cleave, 2002

First published in 2002

06 05 04 03 02
10 9 8 7 6 5 4 3 2 1

British Library Cataloguing in Publication Data
A catalogue record for this book is available from the
British Library

ISBN 0 435 30690 1

Picture research by Sue Sharp
Designed and typeset by Artistix, Oxon
Printed and bound in Italy by Printer Trento Srl

Acknowledgements
The publishers would like to thank the following for
permission to reproduce copyright material: Amnesty
International for the logo on p. 54. Reproduced by
permission of Amnesty International Publications, 1
Easton Street, London, WC1X 0DW, United Kingdom,
www.amnesty.org; The Children's Society for the logo
on p. 40; Christian Aid for the logo on p. 30; The
Christian Herald on p. 40; CND for the logo on p. 95;
Exit on p. 143; The Festival Shop for the slogans on
pp. 73 and 92. The full posters may be purchased
from The Festival Shop Ltd, 56 Poplar Road, Kings
heath, Birmingham, B14 7AG; NSPCC for the logo on
p. 40; Oxfam on p. 34; The Salvation Army for the logo
on p. 41; Tearfund on p. 25, leaflet copyright Tearfund;
Trócaire on pp. 31 and 145. 'I have to make the
journey alone' from Beliefs, Values & Traditions, A
Lovelace and J White, Heinemann, 1996.

Cover photograph by Corbis/David and Peter Turnley.

The publishers would like to thank the following for
permission to use photographs: Andes Press
Agency/Carols Reyes-Manzo on pp. 20, 30, 36, 38, 55,
62, 72, 95, 124 and 125; Associated Press on pp. 26,
50, 67, 74, 91 and 93; Bettman/Corbis on p. 74; John
Birdsall on pp. 62, 63 and 65; Antonio Cabral/CAFOD
on p. 28; Getty Images on p. 119; Hutchison Library
on p. 19; Hutchison Library/Tony Souter on p. 41;
Hutchison Library/Philip Wolmuth on p. 62; Impact
Photos on p. 64; Mary Evans Picture Library on pp. 84,
85 and 90; Mirror Syndication on pp. 38, 112 and
116; Photodisc on p. 18; Press Association on p. 92;
Rex Features on p. 69; Rex Features/Ian Back on p. 87;
Rex Features/Thimas Haley/Sipa on pp. 88 and 94;
Rex Features/Ron Hussey/Sipa on p. 73; Rex
Features/Lehtikuva Oy on p. 62; Rex Features/Tim
Rooke on p. 70; Rex Features/Sipa on pp. 75, 82, 83,
85 and 120; Rex Features/Sipa Herb Swanson on p.
85; Nick Rose on p. 62; Still Pictures/Reinhard-Janke
on p. 144; Still Pictures/Mike Schroder on p. 50; Still
Pictures/Harmut Schwarzbach on p. 87; Wellcome
Picture Library on p. 142.

The publishers have made every effort to contact
copyright holders. However, if any material has been
incorrectly acknowledged, the publishers would be
pleased to correct this at the earliest opportunity.

888058 www.heinemann.co.uk

Contents

Contents

Christian values

This section includes:

- The Ten Commandments
- The Sermon on the Mount
- Discipleship
- Features of discipleship
- Bible passages 1
- Bible passages 2
- Exam questions to practise.

In this section the question 'How should Christians lead their lives?' will be discussed. The Ten Commandments are thousands of years old, yet many form the basis of criminal law today. The Sermon on the Mount contains much teaching of Jesus, including the Beatitudes. They are regarded as rules for living, but are they still relevant?

Many people claim to be disciples of Jesus, but what do they mean? When Jesus was on earth the meaning was clear, but what about today, in the twenty-first century?

The Ten Commandments

Key terms

Commandment Something you must do or obey.

1 You shall have no other gods before me.
2 You shall not make for yourself an idol in the form of anything in heaven above or on the earth beneath or in the waters below.
3 You shall not misuse the name of the LORD your God.
4 Remember the Sabbath day by keeping it holy.
5 Honour your father and your mother.
6 You shall not murder.
7 You shall not commit adultery.
8 You shall not steal.
9 You shall not give false testimony against your neighbour.
10 You shall not covet … anything that belongs to your neighbour.

God gave Moses ten basic **commandments** as a guide to living. They dealt with people's relationships with God and other people. Many people today say they are outdated except for *You shall not murder* and *You shall not steal*. There is an international speaker and writer called J John who is an authority on the Ten Commandments. When he teaches about them he treats each one on its own and churches and cathedrals are packed for the ten sessions. To look at the titles, some might not recognize the commandments. J John says, 'According to social trends, the UK is in deep decline. This generation has lost its moorings, but the Ten Commandments are not obsolete.' He aims to show that Christianity is reasonable, relevant and important, using music, video, poetry, interview and talking. The ten titles that link to each commandment, in order, are:

1 How to live by priorities.
2 Know the real God.
3 Take God seriously.
4 How to stop driving yourself crazy.
5 How to keep peace with your parents.
6 How to tame your temper.
7 How to 'affair-proof' your relationships.
8 How to prosper with a clear conscience.
9 Hold to the truth.
10 How to find true contentment.

Another way of looking at the Commandments is to work out a goal for each one and learn which sins go with it and aim not to commit them. The following give good examples:

No other God except me

Goal To give God alone the worship and obedience he deserves.

Sins To set any person, animal or thing as an object of worship, truth or moral guide instead of God.

No idols or statues of God

Goal No lucky charms, or other such items, remembering you do not pray to a statue.

Sins To forget that a piece of wood or metal is just that.

Do not take God's name in vain

Goal To take oaths truthfully and to keep vows/promises made.

Sins To lie, to swear or to call down evil on a person.

Remember the Sabbath day by keeping it holy

Goal Keep Sunday special, it is a time to worship God, do not work unless you have to.

Sins Missing Mass on purpose, not keeping Holy Days of Obligation, doing work you do not have to.

Honour your father and mother

Goal To respect parents, but not necessarily having to agree with them.

Sins Disrespect, disobedience.

Do not murder

Goal Respect life. To love others and be concerned about their physical and spiritual well being.

Sins Murder, suicide, fighting and anger, hatred and the desire for revenge, drink- or reckless-driving.

Do not commit adultery

Goal No affairs, pure and modest behaviour.

Sins Having an affair, looking at pornography, no dirty jokes, immodesty.

Do not steal

Goal Do not touch or take what does not belong to you, pay your debts, no fraud, do not claim benefits you are not entitled to.

Sins Stealing, fraud, cheating and dishonesty, accepting bribes and damaging what is not yours.

Do not give false testimony against your neighbour

Goal Always speak the truth.

Sins Lies, spreading rumours, destroying the good name of someone else or slander.

Do not desire anything that belongs to your neighbour

Goal Be pure in thought, do not long for things you cannot have.

Sins Dirty or lustful thoughts, which can lead to action, envying the success of others, the thought of stealing.

What did Jesus say?

By the time of Jesus, many Jewish leaders had invented ways of getting round the Ten Commandments or had embellished them. Jesus summed up the Ten Commandments: *'Love God and love your neighbour as yourself'* (Mark 12: 28–31).

The Ten Commandments said:	Jesus said:
No other Gods except me	Worship the Lord your God, and serve Him only (Matthew 4: 10)
No idols or statues	No servant can serve two masters (Luke 16: 13)
Do not take God's name in vain	Do not swear at all (Matthew 5: 34)
Keep the Sabbath day holy	The Sabbath was made for man, not man for the Sabbath (Mark 2: 27–8)
Honour your parents	Anyone who loves his father … more than me, is not worthy of me (Matthew 10: 37)
Do not murder	Anyone who is angry with his brother will be subject to judgement (Matthew 5: 22)
Do not commit adultery	Anyone who looks at a woman lustfully has already committed adultery with her in his heart (Matthew 5: 28)
Do not steal	If someone wants to sue you and take your tunic, let him have your cloak as well (Matthew 5: 40)
Do not lie	Men will have to give account on the day of judgement for every careless word they have spoken (Matthew 12: 36)
Do not covet	Be on your guard against all kinds of greed (Luke 12: 15)

The Sermon on the Mount

The Beatitudes

A **beatitude** is a style of writing found in Jewish writings, such as in Song of Solomon, and in early Christian writings. One or more beatitudes are spoken on a **righteous** person, who will receive rewards, such as family and prosperity (for example, Psalm 41: 1–3).

Matthew and Luke use beatitudes in the New Testament, although other writers use them, for example, John 20: 29. There is a set format used throughout, but the Gospel's beatitudes have one striking difference – rewards will not often be on this earth, they will be heaven. Those who seem down-trodden, persecuted or ignored, are 'blessed', for their reward awaits them in the next life.

> Blessed are the poor in spirit, for theirs is the kingdom of heaven.
> Blessed are those who mourn, for they will be comforted.
> Blessed are the meek, for they will inherit the earth.
> Blessed are those who hunger and thirst for righteousness, for they will be filled.
> Blessed are the merciful, for they will be shown mercy.
> Blessed are the pure in heart, for they will see God.
> Blessed are the peacemakers, for they will be called sons of God.
> Blessed are those who are persecuted because of righteousness, for theirs is the kingdom of heaven.
> Blessed are you when people insult you, persecute you and falsely say all kinds of evil against you because of me.

Matthew 5 has eight promises (nine if verse 10 is separated from verse 11) and Luke 6: 20–22 has four promises.

Meaning

Scholars and theologians have argued over the meanings since they were written. Most say they must be read as a whole and that they relate not to the world's standards and morals but to the kingdom of God.

They can be regarded as a code of conduct for Christians contrasted to those values of the rest of the world.

Other teachings from The Sermon on the Mount

What Christians must be like (Matthew 5: 13–16)

They must be like salt, vitally important, just a few grains make all the difference. They must be like a light, showing the way to God.

Old Testament Law (Matthew 5: 17–20)

The Jewish leaders said that the Torah, the Law, was given by God and it could not be altered. Jesus agreed, but added that what was most important was the way the laws were obeyed and the motives for doing so. Christians must control their minds too.

Murder (Matthew 5: 21–6)

Jesus said that uncontrollable anger/rage is just as wrong as murder. If a Christian is coming to the altar (for the Eucharist) he should make up with his brother or anyone else he has quarrelled with before taking Communion. Christians should try and avoid taking people to court to settle disputes.

Adultery (Matthew 5: 27–30)

Jesus says that if you lust after someone and you are married then you commit adultery. Jesus is not stopping romance; it is an obsession with things like pornographic videos.

Divorce (Matthew 5: 31 and 32)

Jesus said that a man must give his wife a 'divorce certificate' if he divorces her. He knew that many men refused this document, which meant that the ex-wife could not prove her divorce and was still married to her ex-husband. Jesus said the only reason for divorce is adultery. If a divorced person remarries, then they are committing adultery.

Revenge (Matthew 5: 38–48)

This passage is of such major importance that it is discussed on pages 50, 51 and 56. The idea of not seeking revenge goes against basic human instinct and is probably the hardest thing to do.

Giving to those in need, praying and fasting (Matthew 6: 1–18)

When we give to charity it should be done privately, with no fuss about the generosity of it and the sacrifice. Praying is also a private affair between an individual and God, whether alone or in a group. Those who show off, use big words, get excited if people are listening or who do not mean what they say, are condemned. Jesus gave the Lord's Prayer (the 'perfect prayer') as a practical example of how to pray. Fasting is another example of a private action.

Treasures in heaven (Matthew 6: 19–34)

1 Verses 19–21 – You cannot take your wealth with you when you die. Life after death in heaven with God is more important. No one can steal that from you.
2 Verses 22–3 – People will judge you by your actions and for who you are. If you look on life in a negative way, this is revealed in your actions.
3 Verses 24–32 – You cannot be on God's side whilst yearning for material wealth. God cares for his children so will provide for them. Verses 33–4 continue to say that worrying will get you nowhere. God our Father has everything under control.

Judging others (Matthew 7: 1–6)

It is all too easy to criticize someone else and disregard our own faults. Some people do nothing but criticize, whilst often doing the very things they are complaining about.

Asking, seeking, knocking (Matthew 7: 7–12)

This is another way of describing prayer. If we want something then we should pray and ask God for it, as long as our motives are right, for example, we do not want something out of greed.

Christian life is not easy (Matthew 7: 13–27)

Being a follower of Jesus will not be easy. It is a tough journey. People will try to lead Christians astray. They are 'wolves in sheep's clothing', as their words will seem convincing and exciting, but their lives and actions will not live up to their words.

Activities

1 Imagine that you are given the chance to add the eleventh commandment. What would it be and why? **PS 1.1**
2 In your own words, write a paragraph about the characteristics of a Christian, as described in Matthew 5, 6 and 7. **C 2.3**
3 In groups, discuss and agree on ten commandments for the twenty-first century. **IT 1.2, WO 2.1, 2, 3**

Key points

- The Ten Commandments are basic rules for living.
- They are still relevant today.
- The beatitudes and following teaching describe the characteristics of Christians – life, behaviour, words and actions.

Discipleship

Key terms

Disciple One who is a disciplined learner and an adherent to the teachings/beliefs of their teacher.

Jesus chose twelve special disciples to follow him and listen to his teachings (Luke 5: 1–11, 27–32). There were many other disciples of Jesus including women, such as Martha and Mary. What was unusual was that Jesus himself chose twelve disciples when it was normal to ask one person to join a teacher. In the twenty-first century, people are still called to be disciples of Jesus. They might not be able to physically see him and hear him, but they submit to God's will in their lives. The general principles laid down by Jesus are still applicable today.

Life will be tough – you choose!

Mark 8: 34–8 (Matthew 10: 34–9 and Matthew 16: 24–6)

Jesus warned that as a result of his teaching, some children would turn against their parents or a man's enemies might be members of his own family. So the cost of discipleship might be that a Christian was/is hated by his family, possibly resulting in death. During the Roman persecution of the early Christians, many husbands and wives betrayed their spouses, resulting in death – brother informed on sister, son informed on father – so it went on.

If people want to follow Jesus then they must give up their own ambitions and submit to God's will. To *take up his cross* meant people demonstrated their submission to Jesus (carrying your cross to crucifixion was regarded as the most humiliating task a person could do). Christian life would not be and will not be easy, there will be suffering.

Mark 6: 7–13 (More detail in Matthew 10)

This describes Jesus sending his disciples out to do their work, their mission. They are only to take the basics needed, relying on the hospitality of those they teach. Matthew 10 explains that God will supply their needs.

Matthew 16 focuses on Peter's misunderstanding about true discipleship. Jesus also tells Peter about his future work, building the church.

Terms and conditions of true discipleship

These 8 points were relevant two thousand years ago and are just as relevant in the twenty-first century.

1   Follow Christ every day.
2   Commitment to do what Christ asks.
3   Take up the cross – a Christian will face hardships and may suffer for being a Christian.
4   Deny self – follow what Christ wants and not what you want.
5   Take the yoke – a symbol of serving or working for Christ (the yoke joined two oxen together to work, to pull the plough).
6   Love Christ – for example, love might mean forgiving someone.
7   Lose life – in many parts of the world Christians die for their beliefs, for example, Oscar Romero.
8   Live in Christ the Word – this means reading the Bible and praying.

The idea of Jesus having disciples was nothing out of the ordinary. Even John the Baptist had his own loyal disciples. But there were some differences.

- Jesus chose his disciples, normally the student had to find a teacher willing to take him on.
- Most of Jesus' disciples were uneducated compared to the students of other rabbis.
- Jesus expected his disciples to commit themselves totally to him.
- The disciples definitely did not aim to become teachers (rabbis) when Jesus died, they were to listen and learn.
- There would be suffering involved, see Matthew 8: 34–8 and Luke 14: 26 and 27.

Discipleship in the twenty-first century

Christians are to be disciples of Jesus and there are many books, videos and websites to help you become a better disciple.

Jesus walk (www.jesuswalk.com)

This is a series that follows Luke's gospel. It has websites in 103 countries and many regular readers. It reminds readers that Jesus taught his disciples over three years, it didn't happen overnight. Even when he died they were confused.

The focus on this site is to look at an incident/ teaching from Luke, read it, study it, look at some notes and put it into practice. The site does not get into theological debates or give loads of background. Occasionally there might be more than one meaning and if it is important then they will be given. There is an email chat room for students to discuss an issue. Some people only join the discussion forum.

Barratt Ministries (www.barrettministeries.org.uk)

This is based in the UK with the aim to teach basic discipleship and Christian lifestyle. It is based on the Sermon on the Mount. Things like caring for your neighbour and putting others first has, to them, been disregarded and they challenge Christians to bring back real Christianity. The founders travel throughout the UK spreading their story to the world.

Mother Teresa

Mother Teresa is a fine example of modern day discipleship. She gave up everything to serve the poor. She took note of what Jesus had said: *'Those who help someone in need in fact help me.'* She worked amongst the very poorest people in Calcutta. She founded the Missionaries of Charity and took the usual vows of poverty, **chastity** and obedience and also an extra one to give 'whole-hearted, free service to the poorest of the poor'.

- First thing in the early hours of the morning the sisters pray. They may take communion.
- Sisters must turn away from any family wealth.
- They trust God to provide the money needed daily.
- They must be ready to suffer. In Calcutta they may be taunted about their beliefs.

These sites will give you a lot more information:

- http://user.itlnet/mbs96/tribute.htms
- www.gargaro.com/mother_teresa
- www.judithcarino.com

(If you put into 'search' the words 'Mother Teresa' you will be given many other websites to look at.)

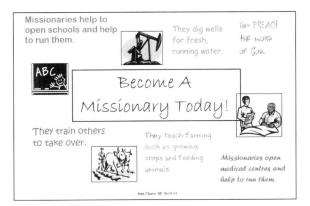

Features of discipleship

There are many passages in the Bible that reveal exactly what discipleship means, what it will cost you and how you should act. In fact, a job description.

Call of the disciples (Luke 5: 1–11, 27–32)

This is Luke's version of events. It should be noted that Jesus chose his twelve special disciples, not the other way round. Verses 5–7 seem to indicate that Jesus performed a miracle. Simon greets Jesus as 'master', which means that they had met before.

Verses 31 and 32 are worth learning. Jesus was there to help those in need, such as the poor. He criticizes the Pharisees in their arrogance for believing they were not sinful.

The commission (Matthew 28: 18–20)

This is before Jesus returns to heaven. He promises the Holy Spirit to help them. Jesus makes it clear that they are to spread the gospel worldwide, so gentiles are included here.

The rich young man (Matthew 19: 16–30)

This story is useful to use in the section about wealth and CAFOD. Jesus makes it quite clear that having money, possessions and other wordly concerns makes it difficult to enter the Kingdom of God. The young man was so nearly there, but his love of money held him down. Once you have had something, it is often hard to do without it.

When a camel loaded with goods arrived at the city gates, the owner would take it to the Needle gate (a small gate within the large one), but it was a tight fit so the goods would have to be unloaded before entering. Therefore, before a person enters God's kingdom, he must get rid of wordly things that hold him back.

The good Samaritan (Luke 10: 25–37)

This parable is also discussed in detail in the section dealing with discrimination. The story had a 'sting in the tail', as the very people the crowd expected to help did not, and the Samaritan whom they expected to finish off the Jewish man, did not kill him. He crossed the boundaries and helped the injured man. Christians have to put aside prejudices and help those in need.

The mission of the twelve (Mark 6: 7–13)

This should not be confused with the commission at the end of Jesus' time on earth. This is their job description. They are to take the bare necessities with them and God will look after them. Some Franciscan friaries are still based on these principles.

The cost of discipleship (Mark 8: 34–8)

Jesus makes it clear that it will not be easy to follow him. The concept of carrying your cross seems alien to us today, but in Jesus' day, everyone knew what it meant. A condemned criminal had to carry his own cross, his own implement of torture, to the place of execution. It was the ultimate humiliation in this case, showing total submission to the Romans. Jesus is saying that to follow him you must be prepared to obey him 100 per cent. If you die for your faith, you will be rewarded in heaven and no Christian should be ashamed of their faith.

The status of discipleship (Matthew 20: 24–8)

The idea of the master being a servant has parallels with the Last Supper, when Jesus washed his disciples' feet. Jesus points out that nobody is more important than anyone else in God's kingdom. The phrase 'lord it over them' implies a kind of arrogance that again, has no place in a Christian's life.

The widow (Mark 12: 41–4)

When Christians give to the church collection, they should not make a show of giving a big amount. The sum of money does not matter to Jesus. What does matter is your attitude and what is in your heart. Is it begrudging? Is it out of duty? Is it given with a sigh? Is it given with a 'thank you' to God for providing things?

The Great Commandment (Mark 12: 28–31)

This was a loaded question. Which ever one Jesus chose would be wrong. Instead, Jesus summarizes the commandments into two: love God and love your neighbour like you care for yourself. Jesus tells various parables to explain exactly the definition of 'neighbour'.

Parables of the kingdom

These parables can also be found in the other **gospels**, but it is the version of each in Matthew that should be learned.

The parable of the sower (Matthew 13: 1–23)

The seed is God's good news and this is about the reaction to it. Jesus describes where the seed fell and what happened to it.

Path	→	Birds ate seed	→	People hear but do no listen at all
Rocky ground	→	Began to grow, but died soon, as not enough soil	→	People hear and believe, but give up at the first sign of trouble
Thorn bushes	→	Began to grow, but soon choked by thorns	→	People hear, believe, but give up because they worry or want more money or more possessions
Good soil	→	Grow well, many ears of golden corn	→	People hear, believe and put their beliefs into action, telling others about God. Some do more than others

Parable of the mustard seed (Matthew 13: 31 and 32)

The mustard seed is the smallest seed in the world, but when it has grown and matured, it is one of the biggest plants. Christianity had small beginnings, but soon grew and grew. The idea of birds nesting possibly means that gentiles are to be included. The meaning of this parable, according to Jesus, has not been recorded, so we have to think of meanings.

Parable of the yeast (Matthew 13: 33)

A small amount of yeast can produce lots of dough, ready to rise. Again, there is no recorded meaning, but it implies that small beginnings will lead to bigger things.

The parable of the hidden treasure (Matthew 13: 44) and The parable of the pearl (Matthew 13: 45 and 46)

People are so keen to enter the Kingdom of God that they will give up everything to enter.

The parable of the net (Matthew 13: 47–50)

When a catch of fish is landed, it is sorted carefully. The useless fish are discarded. Jesus says this is what will happen on Judgement Day – the worthless people will be discarded.

Bible passages

Here you will find some useful passages that you will need for Christian values. It is not possible to print every passage in full, but there will be a selection followed by explanations.

The Ten Commandments (Exodus 20: 1–17)

And God spoke all these words: 'I am the Lord your God, who brought you out of Egypt, out of the land of slavery.

'You shall have no other gods before me. You shall not make for yourself an idol in the form of anything in heaven above or on the earth beneath or in the waters below. You shall not bow down to them or worship them; for I, the Lord your God, am a jealous God, punishing the children for the sin of the fathers to the third and fourth generation of those who hate me, but showing love to a thousand generations of those who love me and keep my commandments.

'You shall not misuse the name of the Lord your God, for the Lord will not hold anyone guiltless who misuses his name.

'Remember the Sabbath day by keeping it holy. Six days you shall labour and do all your work, but the seventh day is a Sabbath to the Lord your God. On it you shall not do any work, neither you, nor your son or daughter, nor your manservant or maidservant, nor your animals, nor the alien within your gates. For in six days the Lord made the heavens and the earth, the sea, and all that is in them, but he rested on the seventh day. Therefore the Lord blessed the Sabbath day and made it holy.

'Honour your father and your mother, so that you may live long in the land the Lord your God is giving you.

'You shall not murder.

'You shall not commit adultery.

'You shall not steal.

'You shall not give false testimony against your neighbour.

'You shall not covet your neighbour's house. You shall not covet your neighbour's wife, or his manservant or maidservant, his ox or donkey, or anything that belongs to your neighbour.'

The importance of the Ten Commandments has been discussed on pages 2–3.

The Beatitudes (Matthew 5: 1–12)

Now when he saw the crowds, he went up on a mountainside and sat down. His disciples came to him, and he began to teach them, saying:

'Blessed are the poor in spirit, for theirs is the kingdom of heaven.

'Blessed are those who mourn, for they will be comforted.

'Blessed are the meek, for they will inherit the earth.

'Blessed are those who hunger and thirst for righteousness, for they will be filled.

'Blessed are the merciful, for they will be shown mercy.

'Blessed are the pure in heart, for they will see God.

'Blessed are the peacemakers, for they will be called sons of God.

'Blessed are those who are persecuted because of righteousness, for theirs is the kingdom of heaven.

'Blessed are you when people insult you, persecute you and falsely say all kinds of evil against you because of me.

'Rejoice and be glad, because great is your reward in heaven, for in the same way they persecuted the prophets who were before you.'

These words have been fully discussed on pages 4–5.

The mission of the twelve (Mark 6: 7–13)

Calling the Twelve to him, he sent them out two by two and gave them authority over evil spirits. These were his instructions:

'Take nothing for the journey except a staff – no bread, no bag, no money in your belts. Wear sandals but not an extra tunic. Whenever you enter a house, stay there until you leave that town. And if any place will not welcome you or listen to you, shake the dust off your feet when you leave, as a testimony against them.'

They went out and preached that people should repent. They drove out many demons and anointed many sick people with oil and healed them.

This passage summarizes the job description of being a disciple of Jesus.

The cost of discipleship (Mark 8: 34–8)

Then he called the crowd to him along with his disciples and said:

'If anyone would come after me, he must deny himself and take up his cross and follow me. For whoever wants to save his life will lose it, but whoever loses his life for me and for the gospel will save it. What good is it for a man to gain the whole world, yet forfeit his soul? Or what can a man give in exchange for his soul? If anyone is ashamed of me and my words in this adulterous and sinful generation, the Son of Man will be ashamed of him when he comes in his Father's glory with the holy angels.'

Jesus made it clear this job would not be easy, there would be a cost, which may be death. Your reward will be in heaven.

The great commandment (Mark 12: 28–31)

One of the teachers of the law came and heard them debating. Noticing that Jesus had given them a good answer, he asked them, 'Of all the commandments, which is the most important?'

'The most important one,' answered Jesus, 'is this: Hear, O Israel, the Lord our God, the Lord is one. Love the Lord your God with all your heart and with all your soul and with all your mind and with all your strength.

'The second is this: Love your neighbour as yourself. There is no commandment greater than these.'

Jesus summarizes the basis of Christian living. The parable of the good Samaritan was told to illustrate the point.

The commission (Matthew 28: 18–20)

Then Jesus came to them and said, 'All authority in heaven and on earth has been given to me. Therefore go and make disciples of all nations, baptizing them in the name of the Father and of the Son and of the Holy Spirit, and teaching them to obey everything I have commanded you. And surely I am with you always, to the very end of the age.'

These words are often said at the end of services, including baptism, confirmation and the Eucharist.

Activities

1 Do you think that the Ten Commandments and the Beatitudes are all you need to be a Christian? Discuss arguments for and against this statement.
   C 1.1, 1.2, WO 1.3

2 Design a poster advertising vacancies for being:

   a a disciple in the time of Jesus

   b a disciple in the twenty-first century.

   Use Bible quotes and consider the qualities you think would be essential and desirable. Are the two very different? **IT 2.3**

Exam questions to practise

Below are some sample exam questions for paper 2B. To help you score full marks, the first three questions are followed by some tips from examiners. Before attempting the remaining questions, try to work out your own strategy for approaching it.

1 'Blessed [happy] are the merciful.' How can Christians show mercy today? (2) *(2B A1a 2001)*

2 Explain why some Christians think that the beatitudes are no longer relevant. (3) *(2B A1c 2001)*

3 When a widow put two small coins into the treasury, Jesus said she had given more than all the others. Explain what he meant. (2)

Now try questions 4, 5 and 6 on your own. Before you write your answers, spend some time thinking of your approach.

4 What can Christians learn about the Kingdom of God from the parable of the mustard seed? (3) *(2B 2001)*

5 'There are no rewards for becoming a disciple of Jesus today.' Do you agree? Give reasons for your answer showing you have thought about more than one point of view. (5)

6 'If everyone kept all of the Ten Commandments, the world would be a better place.' Explain two different Christian opinions of this statement. (6)

How to score full marks

1 There are 2 marks, so you could write one idea and explain it, or in this case, you could write down 2 ideas – remember it is only worth 2 marks!

2 Think how the beatitudes are used by Christians today. You should quote at least one.

3 Do NOT rewrite the story – you will get no marks for this. You are being asked for the meaning.

Justice and reconciliation

This section includes:

- A divided world
- Debt
- Child six billion
- Population
- Education
- Diseases and health care
- Short- and long-term aid
- CAFOD
- Christian Aid and Trocaire
- Exploitation of workers and Fairtrade
- Raising awareness in the UK
- Oscar Romero
- The rich-poor divide in the UK
- Poverty in the UK
- Bible passages 1
- Bible passages 2
- Exam questions to practise

In this section issues of poverty will be discussed, as well as possible solutions. There is an in-depth look at Christian voluntary agencies that help people in developing countries. Additionally, there is a profile of Oscar Romero, a priest who gave his life to help the poorest of people. There is a look at what the Bible teaches about wealth.

A divided world

It is a well-known fact that the resources in the world are unequally shared out. In many areas the rich are getting richer and the poor are getting poorer.

Enough to go round?

Some 80 per cent of the world population have twenty per cent of the resources, and therefore twenty per cent of the world population have 80 per cent of the resources.

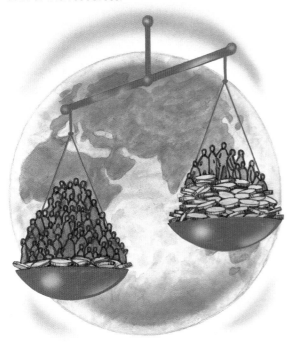

It has been said by several people that we have enough for everyone's needs. Not everyone is greedy. Yet people still die of hunger!

Differences between the rich world and the poor world	
Rich world	**Poor world**
FOOD	
Plenty of food	Very little food
Food is wasted	Every last grain is used
Balanced diet available	**Malnutrition** common, plus
Obesity is a growing problem	linked diseases – for
Food from around	example, ricketts
the world is available	Limited diet such as rice only
WATER	
Clean water	Most water contaminated
Water usually drinkable	Water full of harmful bacteria
from tap	
Each house has running water	A well in a village is a luxury
Separate sanitation and fresh	Sewage mixes with drinking
water system	water
EDUCATION	
In UK, education from age	Many have no free schooling
four to eighteen is free	Rely on sponsorship for
Choice of private schooling	school
All children must go to school	Little chance of education
or good home tuition	for poor children
must be provided	
HEALTH	
In UK there is free medical	Usually you pay before
care	treatment
Choice of private or NHS	No choice
Most people live near a	Nearest hospital could be
hospital	300 miles away
Plenty of GPs available	Doctors may do clinics once
Latest in medical care	every three months
	Outdated technology and
	medicines
HOUSING	
Housing is generally good	Shelter built from what
Houses have water, gas, toilet,	materials can be found
electricity and so on	Usual to have no electricity
	and so on
SOCIAL SECURITY	
Unemployment benefit and	Nothing for unemployment
pensions	or old age

Five basic needs

Agencies have worked out that there are five basic needs for all human beings. They are:

food, water, health, education, work.

Most countries would agree in principle, but some say their country has no money to do anything about it. Others will question the definition of each need. For example, what is adequate housing? A slum to someone from the UK could well be a mansion for someone from an Indian shanty town! Others will argue the priority you should give to each thing in the list.

- *Food*. This is essential for life. Without it the body will die. If you have no food or do not receive a regular, balanced diet you will suffer from malnutrition. If you have no food you have no energy, you cannot work, so you earn no money.

- *Water*. This too keeps the body alive. Dirty water is potentially an invisible killer and can cause hundreds of illnesses.

    River blindness is caused by a parasite that gets in the eyes when washing. Cholera is spread rapidly by dirty water and is highly contagious.

    Agencies teach people the dangers of water that has not been boiled. They also teach people about the spread of disease through sewage.

- *Health*. It is better to prevent disease than to have to cure it. So children are vaccinated against diseases like measles, polio and tuberculosis (TB).

    There is a shortage of trained staff and an even bigger shortage of medicines and diagnostic machines such as X-ray machines.

- *Education*. Most countries agree that a basic education should be free and available to all children. The question is, who pays for all of this? Poor, debt-ridden countries do not even have the money to pay for food. If children receive an education, they have been given the first enabling step to leave the **poverty cycle**.

This helps them to get a skilled job. They are employable. Voluntary agencies place importance on education.

Many people in the UK choose to sponsor a child's education by giving a monthly donation (average cost £12).

- *Work*. Even in the UK, during times of high unemployment people have talked about 'their right to a job', or the country 'owing it to them'. In most developing countries if you do not work, you do not eat. It is as simple as that!

    For a man, it is often regarded as a social disgrace if he cannot provide for his family.

Activities

1   Get into groups of four.
    a   Work out a list of five things you could not do without in your lives. (You can assume that you will have food and water, so you do not need to count these in your list.)
    b   Do you think a very poor child in India would have chosen anything you did? Give reasons. Discuss in your groups or as a class. **C 2.1a, WO 2.1, 2.3**

2   Imagine you live in a country at civil war. You have been given one hour to leave your home or you will be burned in it. You are only allowed to take five to ten small items, which you will have to carry in your hands or in your school backpack, on a 100-mile trek by foot to a **refugee** camp. What would you take and why? Share your list of items with the rest of the class. If time allows you could also discuss any disadvantages of any of the items chosen. **C 2.1a, 2.1b**

Key points

- There are many differences between countries throughout the world.
- What people in the UK would call a 'basic' would often be a luxury in a **developing country**.

Debt

FACT In 1994, the whole of Africa's debt was £5 billion. This has now almost trebled. In 1994, people in the UK spent £5 billion on sweets, chocolate and crisps!

Many developing countries have huge debts. The amount they owe increases weekly as the interest grows. Trying to pay off the **debt** has now become a serious problem for the countries concerned, with tragic consequences for their people. Take sub-Saharan Africa as an example. This region pays back US$10 billion every year from a loan. This is four times as much money as the region spends each year on health and education.

Loans and debts

At the end of the 1970s, oil-exporting countries such as the UK had much wealth which they invested in Western banks. The banks loaned the money to developing countries at low interest rates. The money should have been used to build schools, and set up health systems and other schemes, but often it was squandered and used by corrupt government officials.

The interest rates began to rise due to recession and unemployment. Developing countries began to earn less as prices of export food fell, and there were gluts of fruits like bananas. But they had to pay more for essentials, which they imported.

Developing countries now owe money to Western banks, the International Monetary Fund (IMF) and even their own banks. In December 2000, 41 countries were classed as heavily in debt. Their debt now stands at US $215 billion. In 1980, this debt was only US$55 billion.

The poorest people lose out in order to try to pay off debts. Fertile land is used to grow crops for export only, the farmers starve while food such as coffee is shipped out to other countries. Free education or health care is often ended, and charges made.

The debt grows!

Loans have to be paid off in hard currency (for example, the UK pound, the US dollar, the Japanese yen), despite some countries offering to pay in goods such as oil.

Developing countries have to exchange their currency for one of the currencies listed above. If the value of a developing country's money goes down – which is quite usual – the debt rises as it takes more of its money to buy the hard currency.

Some countries try to borrow money to pay off the earlier loan. In theory it gives them money to develop, earn more money and therefore pay off the loan. In reality it just adds a new name to the debt. They get deeper into debt, called a debt spiral. Often the loans come with a 'sting in the tail' in the form of strict conditions, such as cuts in free health care.

Solutions

The simple solution would be to cancel the debts. It has been pointed out that the original loans have been repaid many times over, and the developing countries pay back more each year than the West gives in aid, loans and investment added together. In 1994 developing countries paid out, in total, US$112 billion more than they received.

FACT The total cost of providing debt relief to the twenty worst affected countries would amount to between £3.5 billion and £4.54 billion. Sounds a lot, but this is what it cost to build Euro Disney.

Jubilee 2000 Coalition – end debt!

Several voluntary agencies, predominantly Christian, joined together to jointly call for the ending of third world debt. They worked jointly – for example, to gather a million-name petition. They also had their own campaigns.

Church on the Hill
PETITION

1. We, the undersigned believe that the start of the new millennium should be a time to give hope to the Impoverished countries of the World.
2. To make a fresh start we believe it right to put behind us the mistakes made by the leaders and borrowers and to cancel the backlog of unpayable debts of the most Impoverished Nations.
3. We call upon the leaders of lending nations to write off these debts by the year 2000. We also ask them to take effective steps to prevent such high levels of debt building up again.
4. We call upon the Fund Managers of major institutions in the rich countries to consider using a fraction of the monies under their control to purchase the reminder of these debts on an ongoing basis and convert them into equity in constructive projects in the Impoverished Nations.
5. We call upon Shareholders and other beneficiaries of these institutions to lobby their Fund Mangers to comply with (4) above and target projects which can be commercially sound, but which will throw a much needed lifeline to people in the Impoverished Nations.

Sign below if you support the Petition
Name _____
Email _____
City _____
Country_____

Tearfund sold badges made to look like a link chain bearing the slogan 'Break the chains of debt campaign'.

There were many rallies in the UK and in many other countries during the year 2000. Jubilee 2000 groups joined worldwide in a human chain in 600 events, where people linked arms and held candles.

Many celebrities gave their backing. Over 300,000 emails were sent to the **G8 countries** delegates when they met in Okinawa in July 2000. One website, 'Drop the Debt', provided news updates.

The UK Chancellor of the Exchequer, Gordon Brown, announced in July 2000 that some countries would have their debts to UK banks cancelled. Welcome news, but the campaign goes on. The next focus was the G8 summit in Genoa in July 2001.

Activities

1   Using the Internet, find out what happened in July 2001 at Genoa summit. Was debt cancelled? A good place to start your research is with the following websites.
   - www.jubilee2000uk.org
   - www.2.gol.com/users
   - www.dropthedebt.org/home
   - www.cafod.org.uk/debts   **IT 2.2, 2.3**

2   Who is to blame for developing countries' debt? Discuss this in a class debate to get some ideas, then use them to act out a role play. You will need eight people.

   Four representatives (banker, politician, trader and farmer) from developing countries meet four representatives (banker, politician, trader and Jubilee 2000 campaigner) from a Western country – the UK. The representatives sit around a table to work out who or what is to blame for the debt.   **C 2.1a, 2.1b, WO 2.2**

Key points

- Debt is an increasing problem.
- Paying interest back diverts money from where it is needed.
- Western banks do not want to cancel the debts.

Child six billion

There are now more than six billion humans on earth today. In fact, child six billion was born some time between June and October 1999. Although the growth rate is slowing down (due to factors like family planning and the effects of **AIDS**), by 2015 it is estimated there will be seven billion people. By 2050, low estimates suggest ten billion people.

Is the earth too crowded?

Is six billion a lot of people to inhabit the earth? In a way it is, because it took nearly all the history of humankind to reach one billion in 1804. By 1960 there were three billion. Only 40 years later, this figure has doubled. More than one billion people are between fifteen and 24 years of age.

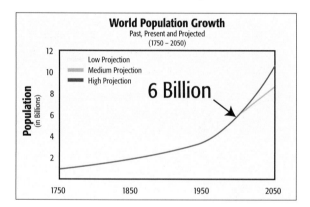

Why the rise in population?

Although nowadays couples are having fewer children, more of these children are surviving to adulthood and having their own children. In many societies the norm is to have families while you are very young. There are two billion under-fifteen year olds who will soon begin having children. Overall there remains a larger population having children, even though family size is smaller.

The world of child six billion

Nobody knows where child six billion was born. It could have been in your local maternity unit! What sort of world was 'it' born into?

- *Child six billion will grow up in a world concerned about air*. Air pollutants add to harmful gases in the atmosphere. They cause ill-health, especially heart and lung diseases, help global warming and create acid rain. Forests and luscious vegetation can be part of the solution. Carbon dioxide is absorbed and oxygen is given out. Many forests are being protected as their importance is realized.

- *Child six billion will grow up in a world concerned about water*. A picture from air shows a world covered in water, but most of this is salt. Fresh water is not limitless and only three per cent is drinkable or usable by industry. About 70 per cent is in glaciers and snow. Some 31 countries with eight percent of the world population face serious shortages of water, threatening health and even death.

  Agencies often get together and divide projects between them. Oxfam is in Burkina Faso in Africa helping a water catchment project, while CAFOD will do a similar water project in Rwanda.

From space, the world appears to be covered in water.

Water catchment consists of constructing sloped areas to collect rainwater when and if it rains. The water is then used to water the new growth of trees, which will later provide fuel, food and fodder in an area where trees have been blitzed in the past.

- *Child six billion will grow up in a world concerned about nutrition.* Farmers try to keep up with the world's nutritional needs. People in rich countries take nutrient supplements, yet there are millions of children with vitamin deficiency diseases.

In many countries farmers grow crops for export, not for local families, to pay off their country's debt.

> **FACT** More than 800 million people are not getting what they need to eat, and the majority are starving.
>
> **FACT** More than one-third of children in the world under five years old are very underweight.
>
> **FACT** One child under five years old will die from hunger (or related illnesses) every 2.7 seconds. How many will die during your lesson?

- *Child six billion will grow up in a world concerned about health* (see pages 24–5). In less than one minute (time it) one child under five years old will have died from *one* of *five* preventable diseases: pneumonia, diarrhoea, measles, malaria and malnutrition.

Malaria is spread by the Anopheles mosquito. It is hard to treat because mosquitoes are adept at building new resistances to medicines and sprays.

Simple prevention techniques are taught routinely. For example, local villagers are helped to get rid of stagnant water areas, the breeding grounds for mosquitoes.

> **FACT** Malaria kills over twice as many people as those who die from AIDS.
>
> **FACT** Malaria is the second largest cause of illness in the world.

- *Child six billion will grow up in a world concerned about housing.* Even in the UK there are homeless people.

Should people have to live in homes like this?

Habitat for Humanity works with the homeless in many countries and has built up an expertise it shares with other agencies. Habitat for Humanity has built 300,000 homes in 59 countries.

- *Child six billion will grow up in a world concerned about education* (see pages 22–3). In the poorest countries only 62 per cent of men and 38 per cent of women are literate. Education is needed to help people get out of the poverty cycle and to promote equality.

Activities

1 Describe in your own words the world into which child six billion was born. **C 2.2**

2 Write a poem about the kind of world you would like your children to grow up in. **C 2.3**

3 Using the Internet, visit www.prb.org/child_six_billion where you will find interactive questions on each issue outlined on this page. As you finish reading each concern, click on the relevant web page and answer the question. **IT 2.2, 2.3**

Key points

- Child six billion was born into a world where people have identified the main problems.
- There are solutions, but they cannot happen overnight.

Population

Most populated countries

1	China	1.237 billion
2	India	1.014 billion
3	USA	275 million
4	Indonesia	224 million
5	Brazil	172 million
6	Russia	146 million
7	Pakistan	141 million
8	Bangladesh	129 million
9	Japan	126 million
10	Nigeria	123 million
20	UK	59 million

Most populated cities

1	Tokyo (Japan)	34.8 million
2	New York (USA)	20.2 million
3	Seoul (S Korea)	19.9 million
4	Mexico City (Mexico)	19.8 million
5	Sao Paulo (Brazil)	17.9 million
6	Mumbai (formerly Bombay, India)	17.8 million
7	Osaka (Japan)	17.7 million
8	Los Angeles (USA)	16.2 million
9	Cairo (Egypt)	14.4 million
10	Manila (Philippines)	13.5 million
·17	London (UK)	11.8 million

Myths about population

Why are people attracted to big cities?

Myth 1

> *Rapid population growth is not the problem it used to be. We should be worried about the effects of a declining world population.*

Population growth is slowing down, but on average 80 million babies are born each year. Even low estimates predict ten billion people by 2050, almost double that of child six billion in 1999.

By 2050, there will still be two billion people who experience significant water shortages. There will be pressure to find more land, pressure to find jobs, and difficulties in providing health care and education.

Myth 2

> *We need not worry about population growth because human ingenuity will overcome problems. New technologies and so on will produce substitute resources.*

There are limits to the earth's natural resources. For example, coal will eventually run out. If the population rises to ten billion in 2050 – a conservative estimate – farmers will be hard-pressed to feed everyone, and some land just cannot be farmed.

Myth 3

> *Rapid population growth has caused widespread hunger and famine.*

It is true that the main cause of hunger and famine has been the inability of people to produce enough food. Food production has fallen behind population growth, most noticeably in Africa. The main causes for this are poverty, unequal trade where farmers do not get paid a fair wage, and no investment in agricultural technology.

Myth 4

Rapid population growth in poor countries means they will continue to be poor.

Population growth impact on poverty is noticeable at household and community levels. For example, children in large families receive less education than in smaller families. Rapid growth in population in a community overburdens sanitation and drinking water supplies, which causes health problems.

But it is not just population growth that keeps a country poor. Misguided economic policies, legacies of colonial days and unstable, often corrupt governments also play their part. In addition, the country may rely on just a few exports instead of diversifying.

Myth 5

Family planning is just a euphemism (another name) for abortion.

Family planning aims to promote reproductive health and to prevent unplanned conception. Voluntary agencies provide contraceptive services (including natural methods) as part of an overall health care service. For example, they provide:

- pregnancy care, training local women to be midwives
- post-natal care of mother and baby, encouraging breast feeding
- detailed information about contraception
- gynaecological care (needed especially by women who have had many children)
- education about HIV/AIDS and other sexually transmitted diseases.

Myth 6

It is too expensive to reduce population growth rates. The UK and the USA spend too much on foreign aid.

In 1994, there was an International Conference on Population and Development in Cairo (ICPD) where delegates voted to increase spending on population projects. It now spends £8 billion a year for family planning, maternal health, midwifery and AIDS/STD (sexually transmitted disease) prevention and education.

It was agreed that developing countries would put in a proportion of the cost. The UK devotes about three per cent of its total budget on foreign aid, as do France and Denmark. Germany and Sweden give two per cent. The USA gives under one per cent of its total budget.

Activities

1. Find out what the current world population figures are. Have these figures grown much since child six billion in 1999? Work out the percentage rise. A good place to start your research is with www.census.gov/cgi-bin/popclock **IT 2.1**

2. 'World population growth has nothing to do with the UK.' Do you agree with this statement? List your reasons. **PS 2.2**

3. Which world problem, debt or population, do you think is the most important? Give reasons. **PS 2.2**

Key points

- Many people blame developing countries for large populations. But in the top 23 nations only eleven could really be regarded as developing/poor countries.
- There are many myths about population.

Education

The Declaration of Human Rights says: 'Primary education should be free and compulsory for all.' However, there is a big *but* in achieving this aim.

> **FACT** One-third of people in developing countries are totally illiterate.
>
> **FACT** In 2000, 125 million children aged between six and eleven years were not in school.
>
> **FACT** In 2000, of these 125 million, two-thirds were girls.
>
> **FACT** In 2000, a further 149 million children dropped out of school before they could read or write fluently.

The benefits of education

We all have the right to an education, don't we? Below are some questions and answers that prove how useful an education is, even for those in the poorest countries.

- *Why get educated?* Education improves your ability to get a job, to support yourself and your family, and to contribute to the country's economy. It also helps you to be involved in decision making.

- *Why are poorly educated people most likely to be very poor?* The main reason is that without an education they will have extremely badly paid jobs, or will be unemployed or just farm to feed their family. In the twenty-first century, education will be even more important in determining poverty or wealth.

- *How does education save lives?* Every year at least twelve million children under the age of five years die of illnesses associated with poverty, such as cholera. If a child receives an education, he or she will be taught hygiene and health care. When educated children grow up they will know how to prevent illnesses like cholera and teach their children.

- *How does education help people escape poverty?* If you are educated you gain new skills. These skills can help you to raise productivity and output, and often gives you the desire to innovate. For example, a farmer in Uganda with a primary education could raise his output on the farm by seven per cent – the difference between life and death.

- *How does education give people a voice?* If you are educated, you often become more articulate in expressing your opinions. Joined together as a community, people learn how to protect their rights to schooling and their land. They can read their rights to participate in the political life of their country and demand to be heard.

An example of making a difference

A nursery teacher went to Vietnam to see agencies working with the poorest children.

The teacher travelled to a remote area, Lao Cai, high in the mountains where the majority of its inhabitants are ethnic minorities. They have their own cultures, traditions and languages. Voluntary agencies are retraining teachers to use teaching methods that are suitable for each ethnic group.

Families told their visitor that they now regard a basic education as essential. 'If you read you can follow instructions on fertilizers and equipment for farming.' 'You can read what it says about the medicine you are taking.' 'Basic numeracy means not being cheated on prices and weights.'

Ways of helping

- *Supporting agencies*. Many Christians believe it is their duty to help those in need. They will support Christian agencies in a variety of ways, such as fundraising and raising awareness.

- *Sponsoring a child's education*. This is a popular idea at the moment. Many groups and individuals sponsor a child or even a whole class.

Sponsoring a child today

How often do you get the chance to improve the life of not just one child, but also the lives of their family, friends and neighbours? Sponsorship costs from £12 per month – that's just 40 pence a day. On average, 80p of every £1 goes directly towards development work.

When you sponsor a child you'll receive a welcome pack containing a photo, details of your child, plus lots more information about your sponsorship.

As well as letters from your sponsored child, you will also receive regular progress reports from PLAN Workers in your sponsored child's country. Many of our sponsors write to PLAN to tell us how much their relationship with their child means to them – some have even travelled to visit their sponsored child and family!

Why do people choose to sponsor a child's education?

- The person believes in the value of education.

- The person is a Christian who wishes to follow Jesus' example and emphasis on teaching.

- It may be in memory of a person's child who died young.

- Parents may sponsor a child as a family project, teaching their own children what they have to be thankful for, and maybe to teach compassion.

- Some schools link with a school that is being supported and each class will sponsor at least one pupil.

Can you think of any more reasons?

Activities

1 Make a list of activities you do every day that require you to read. Then, in groups or pairs, explain how you would do these activities if you could not read. List the difficulties you would face. **C 2.1b, WO 2.2**

2 Write a poem or story about what difference an education will make in your life (for example, you could state what career you want to follow and what would happen if you could not read). **C 2.3**

Key points

- Many children receive little or no education.

- Education is one way to escape the poverty trap.

- Education enables people to have a say in the way their communities and governments are run.

Disease and health care

In a developing country at least half of all childhood deaths are caused by five illnesses: pneumonia, diarrhoea, malaria, measles and malnutrition. Every day 13,500 children will die of one of the above. Many illnesses are caused by dirty water, while others are linked to malnutrition. In the UK many of these diseases are almost eradicated.

Primary health care

Primary health care aims to prevent **disease** before you get it.

Management of childhood illness (MCI)

All the agencies involved in improving child health have developed a strategy to work together. It was agreed that training must be given to recognize and treat promptly the five main causes of children dying. Clear lists of symptoms were written down and treatment grids provided. Rehydration kits, costing 10 pence each, are major lifesavers. They contain sterile water, sugar, salt and minerals mixed together in a sterile tube.

The poverty trap

Every day about 16 000 people worldwide become affected with HIV. 95 per cent of them live in places with the biggest debt – parts of Africa, Asia and Eastern Europe.

The spread of HIV/AIDS is a massive threat not just to individual human beings, but to the futures of entire communities and countries. People are starting to die at an earlier age (assuming they survive childhood). Many adults are dying and they make up the biggest and most skilled part of the workforce. This is devastating for a country's economy – *Who will take over when there simply aren't enough healthy and skilled adults left?*

HIV/AIDS has a long-term impact on the opportunity for children to develop their skills and talents. Children are forced to take over adult duties, as the adult is too weak or dying, or dead. It is impossible for teenagers or younger children running households and taking care of younger siblings to go to school or work. The chances of escaping poverty are dramatically reduced without an education. In order to survive, children are often forced to take on dangerous or harmful work. Many become sex slaves, often for tourists. They also miss out on support and information that would help them avoid HIV. Even those who do have a school place often find there are no teachers well enough to teach them.

Richer countries can play a crucial role in the fight against the virus and the escape from the poverty trap by ending the debt to banks and spending the money on healthcare and education.

> **FACT** South Africa is the region most affected by HIV/AIDS. In the continent of Africa, 23 million people have HIV/AIDS. 1 million of these are under sixteen years of age.

The need for clean water

> **FACT** More than 600 people die every hour because they have no water or the little they have is dirty. That number will rise.

It is predicted that in 2025, two-thirds of the world's people will face water shortages. Some countries suffer because there is little rainfall, but for most the problem is lack of access to clean water.

> **FACT** One in four people in the developing world has no access to safe water. Two-thirds do not have sanitation.

Many developing countries are trying to do something. Some countries set up community-based projects supported by voluntary agencies. For example, Tearfund supported churches in Ethiopia in their water projects. The source of clean water was tested, drilled for and a pump installed. The community felt it was *their* project. They had a sense of ownership, they had dug the well.

> **FACT** When you next flush the toilet, you will use more water than a Ugandan will use in a whole day.

Dehydration caused by diarrhoea

Three million children died in the year 2000. Some 80 per cent of these children were aged under two. The cause of many of these deaths was dehydration due to diarrhoea. This figure breaks down to:

- 57,000 a week
- 8,000 a day
- six every minute
- one every ten seconds.

If more than ten per cent of body fluid is lost, a person will die. There are several ways of preventing dehydration:

- setting up sanitation projects and digging wells
- educating mothers that breast feeding a baby will usually prevent diarrhoea

A DROP OF LUXURY

Everyone should be able to get their hands on clean water.

More than 600 people die every hour because they have no water, or because the little they have is dirty.
With your help Tearfund partners can reach more people with safe water, food, healthcare and other basic necessities. Luxuries they can't afford to be without.

Agencies work with local communities to provide clean water.

- **vaccination** of all children against illnesses such as typhoid, diphtheria and so on.

Activities

1 Using the Internet or a medical book, look up some of the diseases mentioned (for example, malaria, dysentery). Find out how they are spread, the main symptoms, the cure and prevention. **IT 2.2, 2.3**

2 Imagine you are the Director of Health Projects for a Christian agency (for example, Tearfund, Christian Aid or CAFOD). List, with reasons, your priority top five projects. You can do this as a group collaboration, later presenting your findings to the rest of the class. **C 2.1b, WO 2.1, 2.2**

3 List, with reasons, the main causes of poverty in developing countries. **PS 2.1**

Key points

- Primary health care is important. It is far better to prevent illness than to try to cure it.
- Many governments are working closely with aid agencies to improve medical care.
- The focus of many projects is mother and baby care.

Short- and long-term aid

UK specialist teams work to find earthquake victims in India.

Aid is sent to developing countries and where a need has been identified. There are two types of aid: short-term and long-term.

Short-term aid

This is sometimes called emergency aid. It is sent to an area that has been affected by a natural disaster or a disaster caused by people, such as war. The aid given is specific to that disaster. Many voluntary agencies in the 1990s began to work more closely together and in the event of a disaster broadcast joint appeals. Listed below are some types of **short-term aid** provided by voluntary agencies:

- Sniffer dogs and modern heat-seeking devices sent by the UK in the aftermath of an earthquake to find survivors.
- In floods, the UK may send RAF aircraft to drop aid. Helicopters help in taking medics to outlying villages or to assess the situation.
- Shelter needed by refugees fleeing from war or by those who loose everything in a landslide or a flood. Tents are the first option.
- Medical aid at the very beginning will help with casualties. Children and then adults will be vaccinated against water-borne illnesses like typhoid and cholera.
- An emergency operation clears up and buries dead people and animals. This prevents the spread of contamination.
- Food helps to keep victims alive. The food sent is basic – such as rice and powdered milk.
- One idea that has taken off and is used by charities is Operation Christmas Child. Themed shoe boxes are filled with many useful items.

For example, a shoe box for a teenage girl may contain nail varnish, pens, notebook and hair brush. It may also contain a toothbrush and toothpaste, soap, flannel, sprays and sanitary towels. A box for a baby might contain soap, talc, cream, nappies and bottles.

- Water kits are sometimes sent out with purification tablets and filters.
- Dehydration kits costing ten pence each prevent thousands of deaths due to dehydration caused by diarrhoea.
- In some areas landmine clearance teams are sent to clear an area before people return home.

An example: Venezuela

In the middle of 2000, Venezuela faced a huge disaster. It saw the heaviest rainfall ever recorded. Most of this rain fell in the most populated area in the north. The rain caused mud slides and flooding. Whole villages disappeared, as did roads and railways. Within two days, 30,000 people were confirmed dead.

The first stage of aid was the rescue of survivors. The second stage was the supply of tents, medicine and food. The long-term will gradually see the rebuilding of roads and new towns, but with the need to prevent disease. The donation of clothes was a success. Aid workers wrote out lists of medical supplies needed in the short-term and the long-term. Many drugs companies donated essentials such as antibiotics.

Long-term aid

This type of aid will go on for some time, maybe many years. The key aim is self-sufficiency, becoming self-reliant, the country managing on its own, with its population able to decide their own destinies and futures.

There are many types of project but Christian voluntary agencies often work with local churches because they can be relied upon to distribute fairly. The churches know the area, the language, local customs, and are knowledgeable about where help is most needed. Listed below are some examples of **long-term aid**:

- Tools and basic equipment are given to farmers who are then taught modern farming methods. Model farms may be established, run by a local farmer, where farmers can come and see the methods in action. They are encouraged to grow different crops rather than just rice or maize. The key is the sharing of ideas.

- Medical aid is needed all the time. For long-term aid this could be a vaccination programme, or the setting up of a clinic. For example, in a Blue Peter Appeal, people were amazed that they were giving bikes so that doctors and nurses could travel from village to village. The main emphasis is primary health care, preventing illness.

- Building materials are provided. Agencies insist that homes are well built. For example, in an earthquake zone they should withstand minimum stresses. Tearfund has a project to knock down **shanty towns** in India and rebuild with brick or stone and with sanitation. Local people are then taught how to maintain the systems.

- Education is for everyone – for example, HIV warnings and care of the environment. In many areas people do not realize the consequences of what they do. Some clearance projects result in bush fires, wiping out natural **habitats** and wildlife.

- Training is used to teach local people a variety of skills such as farming methods, midwifery, nursing, building, mechanical engineering, sewing and road building. This is sharing ideas and technology so people can do things for themselves. Frederick Lyons of the United Nations Development Programme recently said: 'Increasingly aid will be about sharing ideas.'

- Fairtrade and Traidcraft. This is where growers or makers are paid a fair price for their produce or goods. For example, Cafe Direct ensures that the people who have helped to grow the produce it sells (coffee, tea and so on) are paid a fair wage. Fairtrade products can be purchased in supermarkets in the UK and also in shops such as Oxfam. Traidcraft sells a wide range of goods such as jewellery, glassware, wood carvings, bed linen, T-shirts and coffee. The co-operatives of workers or growers are named in their brochure.

An example: Hunger project works in Peru

It is not just Africa and India that have problems. The Hunger Project in Peru works with Peruvian groups that are committed to ending hunger and poverty.

The first project was in the Yurinaki River area. Links were formed between local governments, community leaders and universities. Five communities began to transform, priorities being to increase income and grow nutritional food. Farmers began to rebuild dilapidated coffee plantations. They tested and prepared soil. They built coffee plant hot houses to bring on coffee seedlings. Families began to grow food in their gardens and keep chickens. As a result, adults and children became healthier because they ate the right food. Surplus money was put back into the schemes, new products were grown and a jewellery smithy was set up.

Activities

1 List the aid that you think Venezuela needs:
   a in the short-term
   b in the long-term. **PS 2.1**

2 Do you think it is right for rich countries to give aid to poor countries? List your reasons. **PS 2.1**

Key points

- Agencies in the UK support projects in a developing country working with groups like the local church.

- Many Christians see the exchange of ideas as the way forward.

CAFOD

CAFOD stands for the 'Catholic Fund for Overseas Development'. It supports over 500 projects in 75 countries. Recent projects include Landmines Action.

Mission statement

CAFOD aims to promote human development and social justice in witness to Christian faith and gospel values. Funds raised will: empower people to bring about change; raise public awareness about poverty and injustice; act for the poor and challenge governments and international bodies to adopt policies with social justice.

Child soldiers in Sierra Leone

Civil war produces many victims, mainly children. Many thousands in Sierra Leone were made to become soldiers, including girls. Many were branded or mutilated to keep control of them. Bishop Biguzzi and his colleague Ibrahim Sesay risk their lives daily by meeting rebel soldiers and trying to get the release of the child soldiers. These two Christians are supported by CAFOD in their work with child soldiers. They receive financial support and help in the hostel for rescued children.

Take Fanta as an example. She was abducted when she was ten years old, branded with the letters of the general and used as a sex slave until she was fourteen. She was rescued by Caritas Makeni, a local worker sponsored by CAFOD. Fanta is hoping to become a nurse, but awaits HIV/AIDS testing.

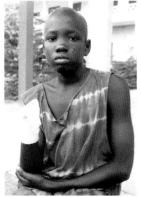

Saving children.

Sustainable development

We all want clean air, pure water, safe sunlight and wholesome food. But the truth of the matter is that we are burning up natural resources and polluting the planet as if there were no tomorrow. Those affected most are the people and communities of developing countries. **We need to act now to bring about change for a more sustainable future**. (From CAFOD's environment policy.)

FACT ● As demands for fresh, clean water for irrigation and industry mount, underground supplies of water are being drained faster than they can be re-filled.

FACT ● The Earth's forests absorb CO_2, produce oxygen, anchor soils, moderate the climate, influence the water cycle and provide a rich habitat for plants and animals. But …

FACT ● Western consumerism is spreading across the planet. In the process, the earth's finite resources are being plundered and the planet despoiled by poisonous wastes.

FACT ● There is more than enough food available to feed every person on the planet, yet millions of poor people go hungry while millions of others eat too much.

Consumerism

The amount spent globally on advertising aimed at boosting consumption topped US$430 billion in 1998. The demand for inexpensive clothes and other goods forced western manufacturers to cut costs. Many have done this by relocating production to countries where wages are low. A designer ski jacket costing more than £100 in the UK would bring the Bangladeshi woman who made it just 51 pence.

Food for thought

When rich countries sell their surplus food at low prices to people in the third world, it undercuts local prices and destroys the livelihoods of local farmers, many of them poor themselves.

Where developing countries get used to receiving 'dumped' food, they are left high and dry when the flow dries up, their own domestic food producers having long since gone out of business.

> **FACT** • In 1998, the UK public spent £5 billion on sweets and chocolate and £23 billion on clothes.
>
> **FACT** • Small cocoa farmers in Ghana supply the UK chocolate market. When they sell their cocoa to fair trade companies, they earn £1066 per tonne and £65 per sack. If they sell to conventional or multinational companies, they earn £600 per tonne and £37 per sack. (There are sixteen bags of cocoa in a tonne and on average a farmer produces five bags per year.)
>
> **FACT** • In the early 1990s, 80 per cent of malnourished children in the developing world lived in countries with food surpluses.
>
> **FACT** • The World Health Organization estimates that approximately half the world's population suffers from poor nutrition and of that half, 50 per cent eat too little and 50 per cent eat too much.

Bamboo – fast growing trees

CAFOD encourages the growth of bamboo, which can be used to:

- convert poor land into good.
- keep soil erosion at bay.
- conserve water.
- provide cheap building materials and firewood.

What can volunteers do?

- They can become parish contacts, organize fund-raising and awareness evenings.
- They could be school/youth workers who teach children and teenagers to understand complex issues.
- Campaign workers support peaceful protests, arrange petitions and increase public awareness about major issues, such as Jubilee 2000 and debt removal.

Legacy of hope

CAFOD encourages people to include a donation to CAFOD in their wills to give hope beyond the grave. Many people do this and regard it like being an organ donor – to give life or sight to others. Other people leave a request that at their funeral people should give a donation to CAFOD instead of flowers, which will die! This, of course, applies to many charities (many Christians prefer to give to a Christian one).

> **Activities**
>
> 1   Use the website www.cafod.org.uk. Find out about one long-term project and make notes that could be used to support an exam answer about long-term aid.
>   **C 2.2, IT 2.3**
> 2   Do you think it is right that CAFOD relies on church donations? Give reasons. **C 2.1**

> **Key points**
>
> - CAFOD relies mainly on donations from supporting churches and support projects in developing countries often run by local church groups.
> - CAFOD brings the gospel of hope to the poor.
> - The 1990s saw a new mood of co-operation, which avoided duplication of work.

Christian Aid and Trócaire

Christian Aid

Christian Aid

We believe in life before death

Christian Aid works in over 60 countries helping people to improve the lives of other people and to tackle the causes of poverty and injustice. Christian Aid believes the following:

- God's design for a new earth puts the poorest first. The **Gospel** tells us to bring good news to the poor.
- Anyone, rich or poor, can be generous and wise.
- Together we can redress the world balance which benefits the rich.
- Loving our neighbours means working for justice.

Commitment

Christian Aid has a vision of an end to poverty, with the right resources to help the poor improve their quality of life. Christian Aid tells the stories of the plight of many so that no one can claim they were not aware of them. It wants to tackle the causes of poverty. Christian Aid works with local churches and those faiths that have compassion for the poor. It is inspired by the Gospel of good news for the poor. Again, this is a partnership agency which works with local groups and does not just give money.

These Ethiopian refugees don't even have the luxury of a refugee camp.

Towards a new earth

Christian Aid is inspired by the dream of a new earth where everyone has a better, more just future. Christian Aid will expose poverty and work to end it, if necessary challenging those who work against the poor. This will only happen if individuals work together. Christian Aid works around the world wherever there is need – working with other agencies to avoid duplication.

An example: Sudan

Christian Aid is working with Oxfam in Sudan, which is still suffering civil war. This has been almost continuous since 1959, with fights over race, religion, culture, resources and government.

- Two million people have died and four million are called 'displaced'. This means they have been driven from their homes, but as they have not crossed a border to another country are not deemed refugees. Two million live in terrible conditions in camps near Khartoum receiving basic assistance. Conditions are worse in the south.
- Christian Aid has managed to get into the south despite intense warfare. Working with the United Nations (UN), its officials gained the agreement of the government and the rebel group (Sudan Peoples' Liberation Army – SPLA) to allow aid to the civilians. There are no long-term projects. War has ended education and schooling, health care and the provision of home-grown food.
- Over three million children have grown up with little or no primary education. In the year 2000, 90 per cent of girls and 80 per cent of boys did not go to school.
- Many depend on food aid, as no crops have been grown. Most cattle have been slaughtered. Displaced people congregate in one place putting a strain on resources like water.

Agencies are beginning to revive projects although some donor governments will only give aid if the fighting stops. Some schools have been rebuilt and filled with books donated by UK school children, as well as pens and exercise books. A basic health care service is slowly being worked upon. As with Tearfund and CAFOD, Christian Aid is part of the Jubilee 2000 campaign.

Trócaire

> *We believe that it is only by changing the structures that perpetuate poverty and injustice, that we can have a real impact on the lives of the poor.*

Trócaire is based in Ireland and is supported mainly by the Roman Catholic Church. People in the UK with families in Southern Ireland (Eire) often support Trócaire. It supports 6,000 projects worldwide, including emergency aid.

Trócaire helped to win independence for East Timor through international campaining and has also ensured that huge companies observed basic pay and conditions in the production of bananas and toys.

Trócaire works with local communities to solve their particular problems – for example, human rights, health care and training for work or community development. It spent IR£13.4 million and IR£8.4 million on disasters in 1999/2000.

This was a popular fundraiser.

Fair play for toys

In December 2000, Trócaire launched its 'Fair play for toy workers' campaign, aimed at making the public aware of 'sweat shops' (factories) in Asia where workers work long hours in appalling conditions for virtually no money to make cheap toys and clothes for the European and US markets.

In 2001, Trócaire will help to rehouse people in Kosovo. Landmines remain a problem. Areas still have to be cleared and made safe before even simple work can begin. Trócaire supports the expert teams financially.

Activities

1   Using one of the following websites, read about one short-term (emergency) aid project. Write notes so they can be used to support an answer about aid:
    - www.christian-aid.org.uk
    - www.trocaire.org **IT 2.1**

2   Borrow or hire a video from one of the agencies and watch its work in action.

3   Using these three agencies:
    - Christian aid
    - Trócaire
    - CAFOD

    divide a sheet of paper into two columns, and list the agencies similarities and differences. **PS 2.2, 2.3**

Key points

- Christian Aid and Trócaire share the aim of helping the poor and bringing the gospel of hope.
- These agencies are Christian, but will help anyone in need regardless of religion, race, gender, colour or disability.
- They are partnership agencies – they work with local communities, groups and churches, and fund their schemes.

International trade for most people is a topic they do not discuss. So long as they get their bananas and coffee it is okay. But if the prices of bananas and coffee fall (maybe due to a glut on the market) it has a terrible impact on the growers, many go in to debt and others may lose their land.

The Fairtrade Foundation

This was set up by Christian Aid, CAFOD, Oxfam, Traidcraft, World Development Movement, the Women's Institute and New Consumer. It was founded to promote a better deal for the poor producers of world commodities and food. It has its own label, the Fairtrade Mark, which is given to products that meet their standards. It does change people's lives:

'It empowers consumers to take responsibility for themselves when they buy food products grown in developing countries. They can choose to buy Fairtrade. In a survey at the end of 2000, there were over two million regular buyers of two or more Fairtrade products.'

Labelling

The most bought Fairtrade products are bananas and coffee, followed by tea and chocolate. Agencies like CAFOD bought items like coffee straight from the farmer and sold them themselves. But to make any impact, supermarkets had to be persuaded to stock these goods.

In 2001, Fairtrade labelling was used in seventeen countries. Products included coffee, chocolate, orange juice, tea, honey, sugar and fruit, such as bananas.

In the UK in 2000, Fairtrade products achieved a sales increase of 57 per cent.

Fairtrade production conditions

- Workers may join a union.
- Workers, including farmers, must have decent wages, housing and basic health and safety.
- No forced child labour.
- The environment must be taken into consideration.

Fairtrade terms of trading

- The price MUST cover the cost of production.
- A Fairtrade premium is paid for investment on development.
- Advance payment facility to avoid small factories getting into debt.
- Long-term contracts to allow long-term planning and to implement new methods of, for example, farming.

Why is Fairtrade important?

Christian agencies like CAFOD believe it is wrong that millions of workers in developing countries do not get a fair share of the money made by their labour, their effort or using their country's resources. This is because huge companies based in the rich world, control trade.

Fairtrade wants to change this so the poor can earn money and improve their lives. The producers will receive a fair price for their skills, effort/time and their crops. They will not be cheated and, with the money they earn, they will be able to afford the luxury of sending their children to school or seeking the help of a doctor.

The producers and farmers are able to get credit to build up the business because Fairtrade provides security.

Exploitation of workers

It is not just abroad that workers are exploited. There have been well publicized police raids on factory 'sweatshops', where workers made copy jeans on eighteen hour shifts for a few pounds in appalling conditions. No workers complained because the workforce was made up of children under ten years old who were all illegal immigrants.

In September 2000, athletes were encouraged to cut links with Nike as they did nothing to protect Indonesian workers making training shoes, gave them no rights and did not pay them a living wage. For example, Indonesian workers were paid about $1 a day – a starvation wage. Workers were stunned when told how much Nike sportswear cost to buy and how much athletes were paid for advertisements. Nike responded by saying that they had done much 'in terms of workers rights, age and wage improvements … they had also improved factory conditions.' Nike said the agencies were targeting the wrong company.

Christians believe they must stand up for the rights of workers. Jesus taught many parables referring to workers. Jesus urged employers to pay on time and pay a fair wage for a day's work. In Victorian times, many social reformers, campaigning for things like better housing, trade unions and better/safer working conditions, were Christians.

Below is a summary of what Roman Catholics and many other Christians believe about work, employers and employees.

- Workers should receive a fair wage. Pope John XXIII said that low wages did not recognize the hard work of the employees, who were contributing to the growth of wealth of the company directors.

- Everyone has the right to have Sunday off. The bishops at the Second Vatican Council explained that this was to enable families to be together and go to church as a family. It was also so that employees could have time to recuperate and relax.

- Pope Pius XI said that workers must work in suitable conditions so their health is not endangered and so that any disability is taken into account.

- Christians agreed that people had the right to own property and that if they owned something they worked harder to earn more money to put into their home. They were, in effect, adding to the wealth of the country and sharing in it.

Activities

1 Why do you think many people are unaware of the exploitation of workers in the UK? Give reasons. **C 2.1a**

2 Why is there often trouble between immigrant workers and local workers in an area? Try to work out reasons for both points of views. **PS 2.1**

3 Find out more about Fairtrade and companies such as Traidcraft. **IT 2.2, 2.3**

Raising awareness in the UK

Voluntary agencies depend on donations to continue their work. Some are supported by churches (for example, CAFOD), while others get donations from the public (for example, Oxfam). They rarely get government money and they prefer it that way – it prevents any political control. Each agency has to make people aware of its work and the needs of the poorest people. There are many different ways to go about this.

This logo will be on display in many charity shops as a symbol of quality assurance.

Fund-raising

Some agencies such as CAFOD and Tearfund rely on churches (Roman Catholic and Church of England for example) and schools for support. They employ people to go and speak to groups.

Christian Aid is probably one of the best-known Christian agencies among Christians and non-Christians alike. In May each year, there is Christian Aid Week when an envelope and information sheet is delivered to every house, then collected a few days later.

Like other agencies, Christian Aid wants people to give regularly, usually on a monthly basis, and hopes that they will covenant the money, so that Christian Aid can claim back the tax paid on it.

Some agencies like Oxfam have shops that sell second-hand clothes, jewellery, shoes, books and household goods, plus new items like Christmas cards and gifts.

Media

The **media** includes television, radio, video and newspapers.

- *The news.* Television news reports tend to be dramatic and focus on tragedies or disasters. Agencies say that once the reports end so does the general interest.

- *Videos.* Agencies use professional video-makers so that their work can be shown. Many videos are aimed at a certain age group – for example, Tear Tots for Key Stage 1.

- *Resources.* These are for different age groups – for example, Tearfund Activ1st is for fourteen to sixteen year olds, with a regular magazine and posters, working for a better world in the UK and abroad. It deals with real people in real countries and cities.

- *Experience.* Something a bit different from Tearfund is Transform for seventeen plus. Transform International (eighteen or over) is four to six weeks living with the poorest communities such as those in Ecuador where you see for yourselves the problems they face.

Using famous people

Most agencies try to be associated with someone well known, perhaps as a patron. For example, Princess Diana was patron of the Leprosy Mission. Sometimes they are active patrons and vocal supporters, for example, Princess Anne, the Princess Royal, with Save the Children Fund for which she regularly goes on well-publicized visits to projects abroad. Occasionally, the association can be as an ambassador, for example, Geri Halliwell works for the United Nations.

Some famous people may wish to become associated with a one-off cause, for example, Robbie Williams has visited various projects in Africa on behalf of Comic Relief.

Certainly the use of someone famous or royalty can be beneficial. Some people will give saying, 'If this is supported by X then it must be OK.' When Princess Diana was filmed and photographed hugging and holding hands with AIDS patients, she did more good than hours of telling people, 'It's safe to touch someone with AIDS'.

Other people question the use of famous people. What about small charities that cannot find a famous person? Do they lose out? Others say that if a person supports a Christian agency then he or she should also be a Christian.

Posters

It is said that posters are the life line of agencies. Have a good picture and catchy slogan, and you are on to a winner. Voluntary agencies now find they have to employ professional advertising people or it could cost them much lost money.

Christian Aid chose the slogan 'We believe in life before death', which can have many meanings. For example, it was put on a picture of a water pump – suggesting that something this simple can keep people alive. And, of course, it is very like the Christian belief 'I believe in life after death'.

Some posters evoke compassion. Others evoke anger. Some aim to shock. Others show before and after pictures. Here are some slogans, taken from different agencies.

- Children are the heart of our future!
- The greatest natural resource a country can have is its children!
- My interest is in the future because I am going to spend the rest of my life there.

- GOD @ work!
- Could you feed your family with a handful of seeds?

Activities

1 Look back at the section about posters and slogans.

   a Think carefully about each slogan. Make a note about whether each slogan appeals to you or not.

   b Either describe or draw what you think the picture would be for these slogans.

   c Share you ideas with a partner or a group. **C 2.3, WO 2.2**

2 Imagine you are in charge of publicity for Christian Aid/CAFOD/Trócaire.

   a Choose a natural disaster (for example, hurricane) and where this may have happened.

   b Find out and list the results of your disaster (for example, houses were flattened) – the geography department may be able to help with this.

   c List the immediate aid you would send and why.

   d Explain how you would raise public awareness.

   e Design a poster or leaflet for your campaign. (If you have a video camera you could video a TV advert as drama – maximum three people in a group.)

   f What long-term aid would be required? Why? **IT 2.1, 2.3, WO 2.2, 2.3**

Key points

- A voluntary agency relies on donations to carry out its work.
- Campaigning has to be done well or the charity will lose out.
- The media generally highlights the bad things going on in the world, but their interest is fleeting.

Oscar Romero

Oscar Romero (1917–1980)

'I must tell you, as a Christian, I do not believe in death without resurrection. If I am killed, I shall arise in the people of El Salvador.'

1917	Born in El Salvador.
	Trained as a priest, then further studies in Rome.
	Worked as priest in many parishes in El Salvador.
1977	Became Archbishop of San Salvador. Used his position to speak out against the corrupt government and against the death squads. Supported the poor people who were getting poorer.
	Called himself a pastor, ready to give his life for his flock.
	Received death threats – challenged death squads to a debate.
March 1980	Murdered as he consecrated the bread and wine in the **Mass**.
Other details	He urged peaceful reform, asking God to overcome the spirit of hatred and revenge.
	He was prepared to give the new government a chance to reform.

Influences on Romero

The Christian ideal of serving others often comes into conflict with Paul's words 'Obey your government' (Romans 13: 1). An example is South America. In the 1960s, many countries in South America were under the rule of military dictatorships. These rulers called themselves presidents and kept power supported by the army. These so-called governments were often corrupt, cruel, ignoring human rights, taking the best land and food for themselves and 'getting rid of' opponents. The rich got richer, the poor got poorer.

Christians in South America, who are mainly Roman Catholic, began to develop a new way of thinking. 'If the church is to serve God, Christians will come into conflict with government.'

This philosophy is called Liberation **theology**. God is a liberator, God sets people free, God supports the poor, God hates injustice, God will get involved in politics.

Archbishop of San Salvador

Romero decided his role as Archbishop was not to be bureaucratic, he was to be a pastor. He wanted to be a peacemaker, ending rebel and army violence and solving the problem of hunger and poverty. In his sermons at Sunday morning Mass, he said that society had to change so children did not die of malnutrition and disease, and so that adults could find proper jobs.

Attacks

Violence increased. Massacres became common, and attacks on the church increased. Priests 'disappeared' and were later found mutilated. There were further attempted *coups* to overthrow the government. People came to his services to hear the news that the government censored. Romero was not afraid to walk in the worst area of cities and towns among the poor. 'I am a shepherd,' he said.

Romero began to tell the world about the injustice, the torture, the missing people and the murders. Some fellow archbishops condemned his outspoken words and accused him of beginning a class war, getting involved in politics.

Romero said: 'We suffer with those who have disappeared.'

He believed he could not keep quiet. Death squads were formed and hundreds of ordinary people were murdered and left hanging from trees, mutilated and disfigured. Romero told people not to panic. He wrote to the American president asking him to ban the arms that were being sent to El Salvador.

In 1979, there was a new government. Romero said, 'We must wait awhile and judge by results.'

Premonition

Romero began to talk of being ready to give his life for his flock. On a brief visit to Rome, he visited St Peter's Basilica and prayed: 'I pray for the courage to die in faith as St Peter did.' It was noted that Romero was a man of prayer and meditation.

He spoke to a meeting of European Cardinals and said 'a church in any country that suffers no persecution but enjoys the privileges and support of the things of earth – BEWARE! This isn't the true church. A preaching that makes sinners feel good so they stay sinful, betrays our Lord's gospel.'

New life!

On 24 March 1980, Romero was celebrating Mass. (Many people now believe he knew he was going to die.) The Gospel reading was from John 17: 1–5 where Jesus said: 'The hour has come that the Son of Man be glorified.' In his sermon he compared himself to a grain of wheat, which opens in the soil to give new life. It had to die for new life. He finished by speaking in general to soldiers. He urged them not to do evil and to refuse to carry out evil orders. A single bullet killed him as he was about to elevate the bread and the wine.

Today Romero is held as a martyr in El Salvador and worldwide. The process is already in motion to have him made a saint. It had been hoped that with his death the opposition would also die down.

But the government was very wrong. Instead of one person opposing, three more men offered to lead the work. Every time a Christian was murdered, two or three more carried on.

A book of Romero's sayings has been published and more and more tourists flock to see where he was killed and buried. He was indeed like the grain of wheat that dies in order to grow and multiply.

Activities

1 Discuss the following questions in groups, then write down your reasons:
   a Do you think that Romero was foolish to get into conflict with the government?
   b Do you think Romero achieved anything?
   c If yes, then what?
   d Do you think Christians today should get involved in politics?
   e Are there any issues that you think Christians should/should not get involved in? **C 2.1a, WO 2.1, 2.3**
2 Using the Internet, visit one of websites about Romero and find out more information about him. A good place to start your research is with www.newmantoronto.com **IT 2.1**
3 Do you think Romero should be made a saint? List your reasons. **PS 2.1**

Key points

- Liberation theology is the idea that the gospel is one of hope for the poor which will inevitably lead to clashes between church and state.
- It is based on Jesus' words in Luke 4: 18: 'The spirit of the lord is upon me.'
- Some people still believe that Romero stirred up trouble. Romero said he was a shepherd of his flock, prepared to die for them, as he did not feel that he could remain silent.

The UK in 2001: divided rich and poor.

There is an idea in some British minds that there is no poverty in the UK. If a family is poor, it is all their own fault. In the 1970s, 'north-south divide' became political buzzwords. Basically the term means that there is an imaginary line drawn across Britain from the west to the east, with areas south of the line being rich and those north being poor.

In the twenty-first century, this myth has been exploded by research and statistics. The divide is not simple. There are areas of both affluence and poverty throughout the whole of the UK. The divide is often described as:

- the 'haves' and the 'have nots'
- the employed and the unemployed
- skilled workers and unskilled workers
- those with a private pension and those reliant on the state pension
- those who can manage their income and those who cannot
- those who save and those who do not.

Characteristics

Research agencies have drawn up a list of characteristics found in many poverty regions:

- A high unemployment rate – 3.7 per cent in south-east versus 10.1 per cent in the north-east (February 2000).
- Poor literacy and numeracy skills – the GCSE score of 5 plus grade A*–C was 52 per cent in the south-east versus 38 per cent in north-east, often due to poor attendance at school and high truancy rates.
- Run-down housing, often council estates – eleven per cent of families in the south-west lived in poor housing versus twenty per cent in parts of London and up to 30 per cent in areas of Scotland.
- Death rates are higher in the north, especially for those in Scotland and Wales. People in these areas will die younger, Glasgow being the city with the highest death rate in the country.
- A high crime rate and vandalism – Yorkshire had the highest rate of recorded offences (March 2000).
- Single-parent families – also characterized by what some politicians call 'an epidemic' of teenage pregnancies in regions of South Wales, the north-west and the north-east.
- Consumer goods – 50 per cent of all households in the south and south-east own a home computer versus 25 per cent in the north-east. Of these in the south and south-east, over twenty per cent of adults are regularly online on the Internet versus six per cent in Lancashire and Tyne Tees.

There are of course variations within regions.

- In the north-west, the Lake District has a death rate 46 points below the average, whereas Runcorn (Halton) is 27 points above (2000).
- Of the top ten most deprived authority areas in England, five are in London.
- Of the top 100 most deprived districts in England, twenty-two are in London.

- Merseyside has one of the highest unemployment and benefit rates in Europe, yet neighbouring Cheshire has some of the most affluent towns and villages in the UK, made even more desirable by the arrival of the Beckhams!

North-south divide?

For most this is just a term, but it indicates that there is a rich-poor divide in the UK.

Sadly, when figures show nearly ten million people in severe poverty, it also means that there are about four million children involved who do not have a voice and who rely on agencies like the **NSPCC (National Society for the Prevention of Cruelty to Children)** and **CARE** to speak up for them.

Child poverty: myth or reality?

The myth that child poverty equalled child abuse is now dispelled because abuse can take place in any family from the richest to the poorest. Some families in the poorest of situations love and care for their children, going without to provide something for them. However, there are still families in poverty where any money is used for drink, drugs or the lottery, and where there is a high risk of a drunken parent abusing the child.

Debt and loans

The poorest people are at risk from 'loan sharks' who lend money with the promise of sorting out debt, then charging very high interest rates on the repayments. This causes the people who have taken out the loan to get even more into debt. Pensioners too get ensnared or conned into borrowing against the cost of their house, then find they have signed it away.

Solutions

- The divide has been recognized so research can now be done.
- There is the aim to reduce teenage pregnancies.
- Many secondary schools concentrate on literacy and numeracy skills and offer vocational courses like child care and mechanics. Many offer more worked-based training from Year 9 instead of all academic subjects.

This is the sort of area which housing trusts can renovate and regenerate.

- Money is being poured into housing estates. For example, housing trusts improve existing housing, and the people have a say in their future.
- The work of Christian agencies and parish vicars or priests is recognized. There are Christians willing to give up a nice house and good job to work with the teenagers, with the poorest families, with the elderly, serving God in practice. They often offer these people a voice, to get their needs heard and to get something done.

Activities

1 What are the characteristics of poverty mentioned in this section? Add any other characteristics you can think of. **C 2.2, PS 2.1**

2 A person wrote the following to a newspaper:

'The poor people in the UK have only themselves to blame! So stop scrounging money off the state you haven't worked for.'

a What is your reaction to this? List your thoughts.

b Do you agree or disagree? Give reasons. **PS 2.1**

Key points

- In the UK, there is a growing problem of a rich-poor divide.
- The actual rich-poor divide is more accurately between areas in the same county or even the same city.

Put an end to child poverty

The Christian Herald, 10 March 2001

Twelve leading charities have joined together to launch the 'End Child Poverty Coalition'. The main campaign is 'Giving children back their future'. Charities involved include Barnardo's, The Children's Society, NSPCC, Oxfam and CARE. A spokesperson said in a statement: 'Extreme poverty affects over three million children in the UK. Child poverty is not a thing of the past. These organizations deal on a day to day basis with the misery caused by poverty. Every day we witness the emotional, social and economic cost. Ending child poverty must be top of the agenda for all political parties and for any government in power. This is not a party political issue: child poverty is simply unacceptable.'

The Children's Society

A Voluntary Society of The Church of England and The Church in Wales

Cruelty to children must stop. FULL STOP.

The young

The facts relating to child poverty make shocking reading:

- At least one in four children live in poverty in UK in 2001.
- At least one in five children are growing up in a home where no one is employed.
- Three million children go without adequate clothing, meals and toys every day. Many of these children skip school as they are ashamed of their poor clothes.
- Two out of three single parents with one child live below the poverty line.

What can be done?

There are many suggestions of solutions to child poverty:

- A strategy to end child poverty (drawn up by the Coalition). There is a need to draw up a national plan for preventing and ending child poverty.
- All political parties must agree on a minimum income standard.
- All people in the UK should have equal access to affordable child care to enable all to work.
- Equal access to the education system, health care, leisure facilities and transport.
- Children must be involved in developing policies to end social exclusion.

Poverty audit

In 1999, the government published its first annual poverty audit. 'The government are setting standards against which they will be judged, tackling poverty and its causes,' said Alex Darling, Social Security Secretary.

The audit lists 32 deprivation indicators and a statement on how the government intends to tackle them. Indicators include poor GCSE results, a high incidence of teenage pregnancies, damp housing, undecorated accommodation, one or more people in the family are unemployed, inadequate nutrition and poor health. Prime Minister Tony Blair pledged to eliminate child poverty by 2020.

Tackling problems

Strategies on how to tackle problems include:

- *Sure Start* – aimed at children up to four years old living in deprived areas. It brings together relevant agencies such as health and education to give a co-ordinated response to issues such as teenage pregnancy, undernourished toddlers, communication therapy and smoking.
- *New Deal* – a programme aimed to get people back to work (many do not try to find work as they say they will be worse off working than they are claiming benefits).

Helping hands

There are people who are willing to help and to give support to young and old that may be lacking in services like the **Social Services** due to cuts in funding.

The Church Army

The Church Army is an Anglican organization that trains lay people to work in a variety of areas such as work with the elderly, drug addicts and alcoholics, and youth work. They often serve in parishes which are in some of the poorest, most run-down estates, in the roughest and most bleak towns and cities.

The Church Army workers who care for the elderly are trained to work in new, imaginative ways and to help churches plan strategies and activities that include the older people.

They try to change attitudes towards older people in society: 'Many people believe that when you get old you become helpless, dependent, frail; lacking in intelligence or ability. People assume that the church can only help the elderly, and don't realize that the elderly can in fact minister to others.' (Adapted from Church Army Focus Group for Older People).

Church Army youth workers try to change the perception that teenagers are alcoholics, sex-crazed and lazy. Youth workers are trained and understand the stresses of twenty-first century life.

The Salvation Army

The Salvation Army is an international Christian church working in 108 countries worldwide. As a registered charity, it demonstrates its Christian principles through social welfare provision. The Salvation Army has over 1.5 million members worldwide with programmes including homelessness centres, schools, hospitals and medical centres, as well as nearly 16,000 churches.

The workers who care for pensioners try to look after them in their own homes, providing basic care, nursing care, home help and meals, depending on the individual needs.

A carer of the elderly said: 'We put faith into practice. We promise, for Christ's sake, to care for the poor, feed the hungry, clothe the naked, love the unlovable and befriend the friendless.'

Help the Aged and Age Concern

Off to lunch!

These two groups now work together in many areas – for example, campaigning. By working together they achieve a bigger impact.

The main aim is to campaign on behalf of pensioners. One victory was the reintroduction of free eye tests for pensioners. They may take a test case to court on issues like retirement dates and pensions clauses.

Activities

1   Using the Internet, look further into the work of organizations that campaign against poverty. A good place to start your research is with the following websites:
    - www.helptheaged.org.uk
    - www.salvationarmy.org.uk
    - www.the-childrens-society.org.uk
    - www.barnardos.org.uk **IT 2.1, 2.3**

2   Do you think some people expect too much help from the state? Do you think it should be 'no work, no eat'? List your reasons. **C 2.1a**

3   How do you think ordinary people can help the poorest people? **C 2.1a**

Key points

- It says in the Bible (in James) that you cannot have faith without actions – this is seen in the work of the Salvation Army, Church Army and groups like NSPCC and Help the Aged.

Here you will find the relevant Bible passages that you will need for the aid for developing countries section. The passages are written out, then there is an explanation of what they mean.

Luke 12: 13–21 (The rich fool)

Someone in the crowd said to him, 'Teacher, tell my brother to divide the inheritance with me.'

Jesus replied, 'Man, who appointed me a judge or an arbiter between you?' Then he said to them, 'Watch out! Be on your guard against all kinds of greed; a man's life does not consist in the abundance of his possessions.'

And he told them this parable: 'The ground of a certain rich man produced a good crop. He thought to himself, "What shall I do? I have no place to store my crops." Then he said, "This is what I'll do. I will tear down my barns and build bigger ones, and there I will store all my grain and my goods. And I'll say to myself 'You have plenty of good things laid up for many years. Take life easy; eat, drink and be merry.' "

'But God said to him, "You fool! This very night your life will be demanded from you. Then who will get what you have prepared for yourself?" This is how it will be with anyone who stores up things for himself but is not rich towards God.'

The man had everything he needed in worldly terms with plenty to keep him going. But death is equal for everyone. You cannot take anything with you, including wealth. Notice Jesus did not say that it was wrong to have wealth here. What he did say was it matters what you do with it. You cannot predict the future.

Luke 16: 19–31 (The rich man and Lazarus)

There was a rich man who was dressed in purple and fine linen and lived in luxury every day. At his gate was laid a beggar named Lazarus, covered with sores and longing to eat what fell from the rich man's table … .

The time came when the beggar died and the angels carried him to Abraham's side. The rich man also died and was buried. In hell, where he was in torment, he looked up and saw Abraham far away, with Lazarus at his side. So he called to him, 'Father Abraham, have pity on me and send Lazarus to dip the tip of his finger in water to cool my tongue, because I am in agony in this fire.'

But Abraham replied, 'Son, remember that in your lifetime you received your good things, while Lazarus received bad things, but now he is comforted here and you are in agony. And besides all this, between us and you a great chasm has been fixed, so that those who want to go from here to you cannot, nor can anyone cross over from there to us.'

He answered, 'Then I beg you, father, send Lazarus to my father's house, for I have five brothers. Let him warn them, so they will not also come to this place of torment.'

Abraham replied, 'They have Moses and the Prophets; let them listen to them'. 'No, father Abraham,' he said, 'but if someone from the dead goes to them, they will repent.'

He said to him, 'If they do not listen to Moses and the Prophets, they will not be convinced even if someone rises from the dead.'

The rich man ignored the problem. He could not say he did not know, had not heard or had not been told. Lazarus got his reward in heaven. We too cannot say we do not know what is happening in the world. We have radios and televisions, pictures beamed into our homes from across the world. We ignore the plight of others at our peril.

Matthew 25: 31–46 (The sheep and the goats)

When the Son of Man comes in his glory, and all the angels with him, he will sit on his throne in heavenly glory. All the nations will be gathered before him, and he will separate the people one from another as a shepherd separates the sheep from the goats. He will put the sheep on his right and the goats on his left.

Then the King will say to those on his right, 'Come, you who are blessed by my Father; take your inheritance, the kingdom prepared for you since the creation of the world. For I was hungry and you gave me something to eat, I was thirsty and you gave me something to drink, I was a stranger and you invited me in, I needed clothes and you clothed me, I was sick and you looked after me, I was in prison and you came to visit me.'

Then the righteous will answer him, 'Lord, when did we see you hungry and feed you, or thirsty and give you something to drink? When did we see you a stranger and invite you in, or needing clothes and clothe you? When did we see you sick or in prison and go to visit you?'

The King will reply, 'I tell you the truth, whatever you did for one of the least of these brothers of mine, you did for me.'

Then he will say to those on his left, 'Depart from me, you who are cursed, into the eternal fire prepared by the devil and his angels. For I was hungry and you gave me nothing to eat, I was thirsty and you gave me nothing to drink, I was a stranger and you did not invite me in, I needed clothes and you did not clothe me, I was sick and in prison and you did not look after me.' They also will answer, 'Lord, when did we see you hungry or thirsty or a stranger or needing clothes or sick or in prison, and did not help you?' He will reply, 'I tell you the truth, whatever you did not do for one of the least of these, you did not do for me.' Then they will go away to eternal punishment, but the righteous to eternal life.

The goats were the ones who got it wrong. They did not help those in need in a variety of situations. Jesus makes a very important statement: if you help someone in need then you are actually helping Jesus himself.

It is useful to learn the six areas of need – no different from today – and what the sheep (Christians) did to help:

- hunger   the person was fed
- thirst   the person was given water
- stranger (a refugee?)   invited (welcomed) in
- no clothes   given clothing
- sick   cared for
- in prison   was visited.

Many agencies try to do these things for people today. For example, some people recognize the Salvation Army working in all six of these areas. Notice that the help was practical, no conditions were laid down and it was not accompanied by any preaching.

Activities

1 What does the parable in Luke 16: 19–31 (The rich man and Lazarus) teach us about:

  a ignoring a problem in your own town

  b what Christians should do when they hear about someone in need? **C 2.2**

2 Look at the six areas of need (in the parable of the sheep and the goats). Choose one area and find the name of an agency which helps that need, listing what it does to help. Repeat for each of the other five needs. **IT 2.1, 2.3**

Bible passages 2

Matthew 25: 14–30 (The parable of the talents)

Again, it will be like a man going on a journey, who called his servants and entrusted property to them. To one he gave five talents of money, to another two talents, and to another one talent, each according to his ability. Then he went on his journey.

The man who had received the five talents went at once and put his money to work and gained five more. So also, the one with the two talents gained two more. But the man who had received the one talent went off, dug a hole in the ground and hid his master's money.

After a long time, the master of those servants returned and settled accounts with them. The man who had received five talents brought the other five. 'Master,' he said, 'you entrusted me with five talents. See, I have gained five more.'

His master replied, 'Well done, good and faithful servant! You have been faithful with a few things; I will put you in charge of many things. Come and share your master's happiness!'

The man with the two talents also came, 'Master,' he said, 'you entrusted me with two talents; see, I have gained two more.'

His master replied, 'Well done, good and faithful servant! You have been faithful with a few things; I will put you in charge of many things. Come and share your master's happiness!'

Then the man who had received the one talent came. 'Master,' he said. 'I knew that you are a hard man, harvesting where you have not sown and gathering where you have not scattered seed. So I was afraid and went out and hid your talent in the ground. See, here is what belongs to you.'

His master replied, 'You wicked, lazy servant! So you knew that I harvest where I have not sown and gather where I have not scattered seed? Well then, you should have put

my money on deposit with the bankers, so that when I returned I would have received it back with interest.

'Take the talent from him and give it to the one who has the ten talents. For everyone who has will be given more, and he will have an abundance. Whoever does not have, even what he has will be taken from him. And throw that worthless servant outside, into the darkness, where there will be weeping and gnashing of teeth.'

Basically, Jesus was saying that if you have a talent (a gift) then you should use it and not waste it. This may mean working for God in some way. A person gifted in languages may translate the Bible into a language where they have never had anything written down before.

Mark 12: 41–4

Jesus sat down opposite the place where the offerings were put and watched the crowd putting their money into the temple treasury. Many rich people threw in large amounts. But a poor widow came and put in two very small copper coins, worth only a fraction of a penny.

Calling his disciples to him, Jesus said, 'I tell you the truth, this poor widow has put more into the treasury than all the others. They all gave out of their wealth; but she, out of her poverty, put in everything – all she had to live on.'

Luke 21: 1–4

As he looked up, Jesus saw the rich putting their gifts into the temple treasury. He also saw a poor widow put in two very small copper coins. 'I tell you the truth,' he said, 'this poor widow has put in more than all the others. All these people gave their gifts out of their wealth; but she out of her poverty put in all she had to live on.'

These passages describe the same events and are almost identical in wording. Jesus said it does not matter how rich or poor you are, anyone can give. What matters is the attitude with which you give. Ten per cent of a millionaire's income is obviously more than ten per cent of a pensioner's. But if you give with the purpose of looking good, gaining publicity or a reward, then your gift is worthless.

Mark 10: 17–31

A man ran up to [Jesus] and fell on his knees before him. 'Good teacher,' he asked, 'what must I do to inherit eternal life?'

'Why do you call me good?' Jesus answered. 'No-one is good – except God alone. You know the commandments: "Do not murder, do not commit adultery, do not steal, do not give false testimony, do not defraud, honour your father and mother." '

'Teacher,' he declared, 'all these I have kept since I was a boy.'

Jesus looked at him and loved him. 'One thing you lack,' he said. 'Go, sell everything you have and give to the poor, and you will have treasure in heaven. Then come, follow me.' At this the man's face fell. He went away sad, because he had great wealth.

Jesus looked around and said to his disciples, 'How hard it is for the rich to enter the kingdom of God!'

The disciples were amazed at his words. But Jesus said again, 'Children, how hard it is to enter the kingdom of God! It is easier for a camel to go through the eye of a needle than for a rich man to enter the kingdom of God.'

The disciples were even more amazed, and said to each other, 'Who then can be saved?'

Jesus looked at them and said, 'With man this is impossible, but not with God; all things are possible with God.' Peter said to him, 'We have left everything to follow you!'

'I tell you the truth,' Jesus replied, 'no-one who has left home or brothers or sisters or mother or father or children or fields for me and the gospel, will fail to receive a hundred times as much in this present age (homes, brothers, sisters, mothers, children and fields – and with them, persecutions) and in the age to come, eternal life. But many who are first will be last, and the last first.'

You need to note the context of the saying about the camel. Jesus had been talking to a rich man who was so near to God's kingdom yet so far from it – his love of wealth stopped his progress.

Jesus went on to explain that wealth can be a hindrance. Once you have something it is hard to give it up, for example, if you have a colour television, it would be hard to go back to a black and white one.

The eye of the needle is believed by some to be the small door within the main city gate. A camel loaded with goods would find it almost impossible to get through. The owner would have to unload the camel and get it to crouch down to get in (the big gates were rarely opened due to fear of attack). Jesus is saying that wealthy people must unload their worldly goods before entering the kingdom of God.

James 2: 14–19

What good is it, my brothers, if a man claims to have faith but has no deeds? Can such faith save him? Suppose a brother or sister is without clothes and daily food. If one of you says to him, 'Go, I wish you well; keep warm and well fed,' but does nothing about his physical needs, what good is it? In the same way, faith by itself, if it is not accompanied by action, is dead.

But someone will say, 'You have faith; I have deeds.' Show me your faith without deeds, and I will show you my faith by what I do. You believe that there is one God. Good! Even the demons believe that – and shudder!

James points out that many people claim to be Christian but forget that they will be judged by their actions. This is a basic principal of all the Christian agencies – words into actions.

Activities

1   Explain one point that Jesus taught about wealth. **C 1.2, 2.2**

2   Explain in your own words why Jesus said it is harder for the rich to enter God's kingdom than the poor. Do you think Jesus is right? Give reasons. **PS 1.1**

3   What do you think 'The love of money is the root of all evil' means? **PS 1.1**

Exam questions to practise

Below are some sample exam questions for paper 2B. To help you score full marks, the first three questions are followed by some tips from examiners. Before attempting the remaining two questions, try to work out your own strategy for approaching them.

1 What does the parable of the sheep and the goats teach Christians about their duty to help those in need? (6)
(*NEAB 2B, B4b, 2000*)

2 CAFOD and Trócaire provide aid to poor people. Describe and explain the sort of work one of these agencies does for the poor. (6)
(*NEAB 2B, B4a, 2000*)

3 A Christian Aid slogan says: 'We believe in life before death.'
   a Explain what this slogan means. (3)
   b Give one example of how these words might be put into action. (2)

Now try questions 4 and 5 on your own. Before you write your answers, spend some time thinking of your approach.

4 'Worshipping God is more important than helping those in need.' Do you agree? Give reasons for your answer showing you have thought about more than one point of view. (5)
(*NEAB 2B, B6c, 1999*)

5 Explain why Christians are often found in developing countries helping those in need. Refer to one Bible passage. (4)
(*2B 2000 paper, B5c*)

How to score full marks

1 Do no rewrite the question. Think about the types of people who were helped.

2 Only write about **one** agency.

3 Is there a Christian belief that sounds like the slogan?

a Explain what Christians believe about helping the poor.

b The example should be taken from your study of one of the four agencies mentioned in the specification.

Crime and punishment

This section includes:

- Crime and punishment
- Aims of punishment
- Capital punishment
- Fighting for human rights
- Bible passages 1
- Bible passages 2
- Exam questions to practise

Many people will tell you that you should forgive a person who has wronged you in some way, but that is easier said than done! The natural reaction is to get revenge or to get even. But when Christians look at the life of Jesus and at his teachings, it is the opposite. In this section we will look at what Jesus taught and what he actually did to live out his words. Also considered is what people aim to achieve by punishment. Reconciliation will be addressed here, including the Sacrament of Reconciliation, which is also included in personal issues relating to the sacraments.

Crime and punishment

Key terms

Capital punishment (also known as the death penalty). A criminal is put to death for his or her crime. The most common crime is murder.

Crime Action that goes against the law of your country, for which punishment is laid down. Also called 'violation' of the law.

Sin Breaking God's will/rule/law, by thought, word or action.

It is not a **crime** to think something wrong;
Bad thoughts can lead to crime;
It can be a **sin** to do a wrong action;
It can also be a sin to think something wrong.

Why people turn to crime

There are lots of reasons why people might turn to crime, as the list below shows:

- The thrill of not getting caught.
- Poverty – for some it is the only way to survive or have anything nice.
- Some unemployed people say they get into trouble because they are bored.
- Drug addicts often commit crime to feed their habit.
- In some households crime is the norm and the children do not regard it as wrong.
- Fraud is often committed because there is a desire for greater wealth than what can be legally earned or claimed.
- Crimes of passion happen as a result of jealousy (for example, a husband may kill his wife's lover), but these crimes are often not premeditated (that is, planned in advance).
- Alcohol causes many crimes such as fights and drink-driving, because drunk people are unable to control themselves.
- Some people argue that children are not taught right from wrong so they do not have moral values.

Electronic tagging –
a tracking device is put round an offender's arm or leg so his or her whereabouts are always known

Capital punishment –
the ultimate punishment, the killing of the criminal (it is not used in the UK)

Prison –
criminals have their freedom taken away

Fines –
sums of money are paid to the court (some fines are fixed)

Suspended sentence –
the offender is set free but if he (or she) commits a criminal act again, they go straight to prison

Types of punishment

Community Service –
criminals work for the community for a set number of hours (such as painting the youth centre)

Caution –
the offender is given a warning and this warning is noted in his or her records

Corporal punishment –
beating the criminal with a birch or whip (it is no longer used in the UK)

Penalty points –
these are added to a driving licence for offences like speeding (if you get to twelve points over a set period you lose your licence)

Loss of licence –
someone found guilty of drink driving automatically loses his or her licence

Types of punishment

There are many types of state punishment as shown in the diagram on page 48. All of them are used in the UK except **capital punishment** and corporal punishment.

Youth Offending Teams

In 1998, the Criminal Justice Act brought about changes to how young offenders aged under eighteen were treated. A Youth Justice Board (YJB) was set up and this oversaw the setting up of **Youth Offending Teams (YOTs)** in every local authority.

Each YOT sends a detailed report annually to justify its multiple resourcing, and to report on targets and performance of teams. One major aim is for YOTs to identify young people who commit crime, especially the three per cent of young offenders responsible for 25 per cent of youth crime.

YOTs form links with agencies like drug action teams and look at data to identify trends such as a rise in racial incidents, or a rise in drug- and alcohol-related crime.

There is a list of common offences committed by young offenders, which includes:

- violence against person
- sexual offence
- death or injury by reckless driving
- robbery and handling
- burglary
- vehicle theft
- fraud and forgery
- arson and criminal damage
- drugs offence
- racial incidents
- breach of orders.

Detailed notes are recorded for the YOT who will often come to the police station to try to prevent the offender being put into custody, seeking alternative punishment.

Activities

1 Find out what the seven deadly sins are. Write down what you think each means. Try looking on these websites for help: www.mission.com www.deadlysins.com. **IT 2.1, 2.2**

2 Take a blank sheet of paper and divide it into three vertical columns.
  a In the first column, list all different crimes you can think of.
  b In the second column, write down what you consider a suitable punishment for each of those crimes.
  c In the third column write down what the punishment would be in UK today for each crime. **PS 2.1, 2.2**

3 Take a look at www.positiveparenting.com which lists alternatives to smacking children.
  a Is it ever right to smack a child? Give reasons.
  b Are there situations when it is wrong to smack a child? Write down what you think Christians would say (for example, some Christians say that smacking children leads to beating adults). **IT 2.1, 2.2**

Key points

- A sin breaks the law of God.
- A crime breaks the law of a country.
- A crime can be a sin – for example, murder. But a sin need not be a crime – for example, jealousy.

Aims of punishment

When a person is punished there is a reason behind it. There are five main **aims of punishment**, which means that there is an expected outcome after punishment such as reforming (changing) the person.

The five aims of punishment

- *Protection*. Society must be protected from criminals like murderers. Some criminals need to be protected from vigilantes. Prison is the usual institution. Criminals lose their freedom.

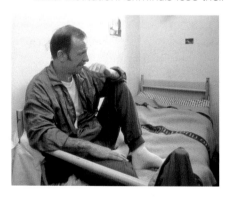

Prisons keep criminals away from the public.

- *Retribution (revenge)*. This is based on the Old Testament principle of 'an eye for eye, a tooth for tooth'. The punishment fits the crime. This is often applied to capital punishment – a life for a life. In the USA, members of the victim's family are invited to watch the killer die, to see justice done. Many Christians still believe this principle is valid and fair in the twenty-first century.

Death Row: in the USA you can be put to death for killing someone else.

- *Deterrence*. The aim is to put off a criminal from re-offending, and therefore being punished again. The other part of the aim is to put off would-be criminals who see the punishment and decide that crime is not worth the risk. For example, in some countries thieves have their left hands cut off. Or, if you drink alcohol then drive your car, you lose your licence and in future will find it difficult and costly to get insurance.

- *Reform (rehabilitation)*. This is often called the Christian aim because it is based on Jesus' words. He taught that instead of seeking revenge you should forgive and love your enemies. Criminals may repent, say sorry and try to put things right (see, for example, Luke 19: 1–10 which tells the story of Zacchaeus).

- *Vindication*. This shows society that law breaking will not be tolerated. The law is to be respected and if you break it you will be punished.

Christian aim of punishment

One aim of punishment favoured by Christians is reform. The aim is that wrong-doers should realize and understand what they have done wrong.

In his teachings and actions, Jesus never said a person should not be punished, but he did forgive them their sins. He also stressed that **repentance** means being sorry for what you have done wrong, putting things right and not making the same mistakes again.

The Sacrament of Reconciliation

The Sacrament of Reconciliation is a sacrament used by Roman Catholics. It is an outward ritual with a holy meaning, bringing people closer to God. The person who receives this sacrament is called the penitent. The penitent comes into the church and prays in silence to God for help, thinking about what is wrong. The penitent then goes to the priest, who may be in a confessional, where the two people are separated, or they sit facing each other.

The penitent tells the priest what wrong has been done. The priest may discuss the situation and then he gives a penance, usually to fit the sin. For example, if the person has been greedy, the priest may ask the penitent to donate money to CAFOD. The priest says words of **absolution**: 'May God give you pardon and peace and I absolve you from your sins.'

There is a similar service where people come together in church. They confess to God in silence, not to the priest, who then absolves everyone at the same time.

The spiritual effects of the Sacrament of Penance are:

- **reconciliation** with God
- reconciliation with the Church
- reconciliation with people who have been upset or harmed.
- remission of eternal punishment incurred by sins
- the individuals should be determined not to do wrong again
- we should all be more understanding towards other people who sin, just like us.

The Church teaches

The Church has the power to forgive all sins. This forgiveness of sins is a true sacrament instituted by Christ. Sins are forgiven only by the Sacrament of Penance. Sins are forgiven by absolution, which can only be given by an authorized priest.

Confession must cover all sins committed since baptism and not previously confessed. The effect of this Sacrament is reconciliation with God.

Act of Contrition (being sorry)

This is an example of a prayer which Christians can use to say sorry.

> 'O my God, I am heartily sorry for having offended You, and I detest all my sins, because of Your just punishment, but most of all because they offend You, my God, who is All-good and deserving of all my love. I firmly resolve with the help of Your grace, to sin no more and to avoid occasions of sin.'

Activities

1. Which punishment do you think is the most effective? List your reasons for thinking this. **C 2.1a**

2. Divide a sheet of paper into two vertical columns.
   a. In the first column, list the five aims of punishment.
   b. In the second column, by each aim, write examples of the types of punishment (for example, deterrence – prison). **PS 2.1**

3. Re-read the section on types of punishment (see pages 48–9). Do you agree that reform is the Christian aim of punishment? Give reasons for your answer. **C 2.1a**

Key points

- There are five main aims of punishment. It is difficult to select the most effective aim as different things suit different people.
- There are ceremonies where you can openly show your repentance.
- Jesus never said you should not be punished.

Capital punishment

Key terms

Capital punishment Also called the death penalty. A criminal is put to death for their crime.

Martyrs People who die, or are prepared to die, for their beliefs.

Capital punishment is an emotive issue. There are few who do not have an opinion on it. It seems most people are either for it or against it. This applies to Christians, too, and both sides use Bible passages to support their views.

Capital punishment is not used in Britain. But it is used in some states in the USA. The criminal is put to death usually by lethal injection or the electric chair. In some countries in South America and Africa, political opponents are condemned to death without trial. This is seen as misuse of capital punishment.

The case for capital punishment

Christians who support capital punishment quote the Old Testament principle of 'an eye for eye, a tooth for tooth' – also called the principle of revenge, or fair and equal justice. So, if you kill, you are then killed. Society will be protected if a murderer, for example, is put to death. There is no chance of re-offending.

Some people are not sorry for their crimes and if released from prison might re-offend. Some seek out former victims or their families to get revenge for being sent to prison. Some rapists get a thrill from stalking former victims, before they strike again.

Capital punishment is a deterrent. Would-be murderers, for example, see the penalty for killing and may decide not to commit the crime as a result.

Some criminals say they would prefer to die rather than live in solitary confinement, which is a likely punishment for their horrific crimes. Some Christians would argue it is inhumane to keep someone on his or her own (even for his or her safety).

Some people have more extreme views. They would say capital punishment is cheaper than keeping the criminals in prison for life.

In many countries 'life' no longer means life (dying in prison). Most criminals are entitled to apply for parole, although judges do have the right to recommend a minimum sentence. But it is quite rare to actually give a life sentence and mean it.

Therefore, some Christians say that capital punishment is the only effective punishment for crimes like murder.

The case against capital punishment

Jesus changed the Old Testament principle of 'an eye for eye' by adding: 'I tell you, love your enemies and pray for them.' Jesus then said that a Christian should 'turn the other cheek' (Matthew 5). So revenge should no longer be sought by Christians.

Many Christians say that capital punishment does not give the criminal a chance to repent (although in the USA criminals can be on **Death Row** for several years). Once you have killed someone, you cannot bring him or her back if he or she is found later to be innocent.

People tend to look at crime rates, especially murders, in areas where there is the death penalty. In the USA the death penalty as a deterrent does not work. Most people carry guns regardless of whether they intend to commit a crime. Also, there are more murders per capita than in other countries. The police say many murders are drug-related or crimes of passion.

Capital punishment turns the executioner into a murderer (two wrongs do not make a right), and this greatly concerns the church.

Some of those executed often become **martyrs** – especially if they are **terrorists**. They are dying for their cause and media coverage will promote their information round the world.

Christians believe that all life is sacred and only God can give, and therefore take, life. Capital punishment goes against the commandment 'Do not kill'.

Right or wrong?

Some would say that if you use the Old Testament to support the death penalty for murder, the death penalty should also be used for cursing your parents, blasphemy and adultery, among several examples in Leviticus 20: 9–10. In the issue of capital punishment, there are no right or wrong answers. It comes down to a matter of personal conscience. Below are two organizations that support opposing views.

ACLU death penalty campaign
www.aclu.org/death-penalty/

ACLU (American Civil Liberties Union) campaigns for the abolition of the death penalty in the USA. It states that there are 3,500 inmates on Death Row. Most are poor people and a high proportion of them are coloured people.

On interviewing these inmates it was found that most of them were inadequately or incompetently represented at their trials. ACLU also reports that since 1976, when the death penalty was reinstated in the USA, out of every eight people sentenced to death one has been found completely innocent. Most of these people were fortunate that they were exonerated before their execution, but some have died. ACLU wants all executions stopped.

Pro-death penalty
www.prodeathpenalty.com

This site was developed to give supporters of the death penalty information that is reliable.

Research has shown that there is a lot of information about the inmates on Death Row – at present 3,500 – but there is very little if anything about the victims.

This website proposes to list the victims in its database. Because many of the murderers were multiple killers, it is estimated there will be about 6,000 victims. The site will have their name, age and how they died, then the name of their murderer. It also gives up-to-date news items about murder and rape cases.

The Church of England
The death penalty was last discussed by the Church of England in 1983. It agreed it would deplore the reintroduction of the death penalty in the UK.

Activities

1. Make a list of crimes that you think should be punished by capital punishment. Justify what you choose. If you think no crime should be punished in this way, justify why. Then compare your findings with someone else in your class. You could make a graph of all the choices in your class and find out which crime (if any) requires the death penalty.
   C 2.1a, C 2.3, WO 2.3

2. There are different types of murder, such as manslaughter, premeditated and crime of passion. But surely 'murder is murder'? Do you agree? Give reasons. Then list what the Christian response might be.
   C 2.1a, 2.3

3. Do you think it is right that relatives of murder victims can watch the killer die (as in the USA)? What do you think Christians would say? Discuss in groups, then outline your reasons to the rest of the class.
   C 2.1a, WO 2.2

Key points

- Capital punishment, also called the death penalty, is an emotive subject.
- There is teaching in the Bible which is used both for and against capital punishment.
- The USA still has the death penalty, but the police say there is no reduction in murders and that the death penalty is not a deterrent.

Fighting for human rights

This topic takes a look at the work of Amnesty International and Saint Maximillian Kolbe.

Amnesty International

Amnesty International is probably the most well-known organization that campaigns relentlessly on behalf of prisoners throughout the world. It encompasses Christians of all denominations as well as non-Christians and campaigns in the spirit of forgiveness.

Amnesty International was launched in 1961 by Peter Benenson, after he read about two Portuguese students who had been sentenced to seven years in prison because they raised their glasses in support of freedom. Benenson used an ancient Chinese proverb and it inspired his choice of symbol – a candle in barbed wire.

The inspiration for Amnesty International's symbol
It is better to light a candle,
Than to curse the darkness.

Benenson wrote an article for the press called 'The Forgotten Prisoners, prisoners who have had no trial or charge'. He immediately received more than 1,000 pledges of active support. Within a year Amnesty International had:

- sent delegations to four countries to speak on behalf of prisoners
- taken up 210 cases
- set up branches in seven countries after just two years.

The main principle is one of impartiality and independence, campaigning for human rights. Members may not become involved in cases in their own countries. In the year 2000/2001 there are over one million active members.

Amnesty International campaigns for different cases. Here are some of them.

- Stamping out torture – ending the torture of soldiers and civilians.

- Joining with ACAT (Christians Against Torture) in a campaign against executions and torture.
- A campaign to stop the illegal sale of UK arms and weapons to undemocratic countries – especially within Africa and former Soviet Union states.
- A campaign to stop the persecution of **conscientious objectors** in Greece, Turkey and Armenia.
- A campaign to improve prison conditions in many countries – such as in Korea.
- A campaign for basic human rights for children, including a ban on the use of children as soldiers.
- A general campaign to free Chinese students imprisoned for demanding basic human rights. Western governments are accused of virtually ignoring the Tiananmen Square Massacre in the name of trade.

One tactic is to encourage mass letter-writing and emails to governments in protest, and also to the prisoners and hostages to let them know someone cares.

Saint Maximillian Kolbe

The story of Kolbe is one of the ultimate sacrifice – giving your life to save another. It has parallels to the death and resurrection of Jesus.

Kolbe was born in 1894 in Poland to a poor family who were devout Roman Catholics. He became a devout Roman Catholic as a young man and helped the local church. In 1910, he joined a Franciscan Order, went to Rome to study and became a priest in 1918.

As a priest he realized that many people were openly against Roman Catholicism. In 1927, Kolbe set up an evangelization centre near Warsaw and sent leaflets to millions of people. He edited a monthly magazine and began a radio station, all with the aim of spreading Roman Catholicism.

World War II began and Roman Catholics in Poland were the targets of German hatred. In 1939 and 1941, Kolbe was arrested on suspicion of helping Jews and of simply being a Roman Catholic.

Not only was Kolbe wrongly imprisoned, but also he gave his life to save another.

In May 1941, Kolbe and 320 others were sent to Auschwitz Concentration Camp. Kolbe shared his rations with others, heard confessions and held Mass. He encouraged fellow prisoners to forgive the Nazis and let good win over evil. 'Hate is not creative. Our sorrow is necessary that those who live after us may be happy.' It was noted that Kolbe always put himself last when treated for ailments by a doctor. One doctor said he saw 'the virtues of Jesus in this servant of God'.

One day, a fellow prisoner escaped. The remaining men in his block were made to stand all day in the sun without water. By evening the prisoner was still free. Commandant Fritsch decided ten men would die for the who had one escaped. One man, Francis Gajowniczek, pleaded to be let off as he had a young family dependent on him. Kolbe came forward and said he would take the man's place: 'I have no wife or children.'

The ten men were sent to the starvation bunker. We have exact details because the interpreter and manager of the bunker was impressed by Kolbe and his faith, and he wrote notes in his diary. Each day soldiers removed the bodies of the dead. They noticed a calm in the bunker, with Kolbe leading the remaining men in the singing of hymns and prayers.

The interpreter used to go in and talk to the starving men, amazed at how calm they were.

He noted that none of them had turned to cannibalism.

Two weeks later only Kolbe and three others were left and the bunker was needed for more men. Each man was injected with carbolic acid and Kolbe was made to watch. Then it was his turn. He raised his arm and he was injected, yet he did not die. He simply seemed calm and peaceful. He was injected again and appeared to fall asleep. The date was 14 August 1941.

In 1982, Kolbe was canonized (enrolled in the list of saints) by Pope John Paul II. He was now a saint and martyr. The family of the man whose life was spared attended the ceremony.

Activities

1   Using the Internet, visit the Amnesty website (www.amnesty.org.uk). Choose one area in which this organization works and find out more about it (for example, trying to ban and rescue child soldiers). Then give a presentation to the rest of your class.
    C 2.1b, IT 2.2

2   For many Christians, Kolbe is a martyr and a hero. But to some he is a fool. What do you think? List your reasons. **C 2.2**

3   Imagine you are Francis, the man who was spared. You have just been set free and you write a letter to your wife and children saying you are coming home. Give details in your letter on how your life was spared and what your feelings are. **C 2.2, 2.3**

Key points

- There are still many people throughout the world who are falsely imprisoned, without charge, and without trial.

- Amnesty International and other groups campaign for the basic human rights of prisoners. They work in the spirit of reconciliation.

- Saint Kolbe was imprisoned and gave his life to save a fellow human being.

Here you will find the relevant Bible passages that you will need for the crime and punishment section. The passages are written out, then there is an explanation of what they mean. Following that are some extra passages that you can learn and use in the exam. You will be given credit for using additional biblical material.

> **It is very important to note that Jesus never said, or even hinted, that you should not be punished. What he did say was that the sinner should be forgiven and given the chance to reform.**

Matthew 5: 38–48 (Teaching on forgiveness)

You have heard that it was said 'Eye for eye, and tooth for tooth'. But I tell you, Do not resist an evil person. If someone strikes you on the right cheek, turn to him the other also. And if someone wants to sue you and take your tunic, let him have your cloak as well. If someone forces you to go one mile, go with him two miles. Give to the one who asks you, and do not turn away from the one who wants to borrow from you. You have heard that it was said, 'Love your neighbour and hate your enemy.' But I tell you: Love your enemies and pray for those who persecute you, that you may be sons of your Father in heaven. He causes his sun to shine on the evil and the good, and sends rain on the righteous and the unrighteous. If you love those who love you, what reward will you get? Are not even the tax collectors doing that? And if you greet only your brothers, what are you doing more than others? Do not even pagans do that? Be perfect, therefore, as your heavenly Father is perfect.

Jesus quotes the Old Testament principle of fair revenge *but* adds to it by saying 'but I tell you do not take revenge'. Jesus turns the principle round.

He goes on to talk about 'turning the other cheek'. This takes courage, as the natural human reaction is one of retaliation. But it is important to understand that it is not pretending the problem does not exist and ignoring it – hoping it will go away, head-in-sand syndrome. Rather, it is seeking other ways of solving the problem and calming the immediate situation. Loving your enemies is difficult in practice, but Jesus makes clear he wants his followers to be different. They should 'stand out in the crowd'.

Luke 15: 11–32 (The forgiving father)

Jesus continued: 'There was a man who had two sons. The younger one said to his father, "Father, give me my share of the estate." So he divided his property between them.

'Not long after that, the younger son got together all he had, set off for a distant country and there squandered his wealth in wild living. After he had spent everything, there was a severe famine in that whole country, and he began to be in need. So he went and hired himself out to a citizen of that country, who sent him to his fields to feed pigs. He longed to fill his stomach with the pods that the pigs were eating, but no-one gave him anything.

'When he came to his senses, he said, "How many of my father's hired men have food to spare, and here I am starving to death! I will set out and go back to my father and say to him: Father, I have sinned against heaven and against you. I am no longer worthy to be called your son; make me like one of your hired men." So he got up and went to his father.

'But while he was still a long way off, his father saw him and was filled with compassion for him; he ran to his son, threw his arms around him and kissed him. The son said to him, "Father, I have sinned against heaven and against you. I am no longer worthy to be called your son."

'But the father said to his servants. "Quick! Bring the best robe and put it on him. Put a ring on his finger and sandals on his feet.

Bring the fattened calf and kill it. Let's have a feast and celebrate! For this son of mine was dead and is alive again; he was lost and is found!" So they began to celebrate.

'Meanwhile, the older son was in the field. When he came near the house, he heard music and dancing. So he called one of the servants and asked him what was going on. "Your brother has come," he replied, "and your father has killed the fattened calf because he has him back safe and sound." The older brother became angry and refused to go in. So his father went out and pleaded with him. But he answered his father, "Look! All these years I've been slaving for you and never disobeyed your orders. Yet you never gave me even a young goat so I could celebrate with my friends! But when this son of yours who has squandered your property with prostitutes comes home, you kill the fattened calf for him!"

'"My son," the father answered, "you are always with me, and everything I have is yours. But we had to celebrate and be glad, because this brother of yours was dead and is alive again; he was lost and is found."'

This parable is also called 'The prodigal son' or 'The lost son', but in this exam it is called 'The forgiving father'. There are several meanings to this parable.

- The father represents God and the story teaches us about how God loves to forgive. The father is shown waiting for his son, hoping that one day he will come home. He knew what would happen but he let his son go, to make his own decisions, to learn from his mistakes. God has given us free will. We all sin but God waits for us, ready to forgive. When the son came home, the father celebrated. He did not say, 'I told you so.'

- The second son was given a choice and he made the wrong one. It took a long while for him to realize his misdeeds and the error of his ways. In the end, he was prepared to become a servant and lose his status as son.

- The elder son represents the Jewish leaders who objected to outcasts, poor people, the sick and 'sinful' people being forgiven. They realized that Jesus' message showed they were hypocritical. The Jewish leaders thought that some people were just too sinful to be forgiven.

Christians learn about God who is their father. He is willing to forgive those who repent. Christians try to live like Jesus, so they too must forgive those who repent. This may mean letting go of grudges and not being annoyed that someone is being given a second chance.

Mark 2: 1–12 (The paralyzed man)

A few days later, when Jesus again entered Capernaum, the people heard that he had come home. So many gathered that there was no room left, not even outside the door, and he preached the word to them.

Some men came, bringing to him a paralytic, carried by the four of them. Since they could not get him to Jesus because of the crowd, they made an opening in the roof above Jesus and, after digging through it, lowered the mat the paralyzed man was lying on.

When Jesus saw their faith, he said to the paralytic, 'Son, your sins are forgiven.'

Now some teachers of the law were sitting there, thinking to themselves, 'Why does this fellow talk like that? He's blaspheming! Who can forgive sins but God alone?'

Immediately Jesus knew in his spirit that this is what they were thinking in their hearts, and he said to them, 'Why are you thinking these things? Which is easier: to say to the paralytic "Your sins are forgiven", or to say, "Get up, take your mat and walk"? But that you may know that the Son of Man has authority on earth to forgive sins …' He said to the paralytic, 'I tell you, get up, take your mat and go home.'

He got up, took his mat and walked out in full view of them all. This amazed everyone and they praised God, saying, 'We have never seen anything like this!

In the time of Jesus the belief was that if you sinned you would be punished with illness. (Some people in the twenty-first century still believe this, for example, some people say that AIDS is a punishment for casual sex.) When Jesus healed the man he also forgave his sins. The crowd heard Jesus forgive his sins so he could be healed.

Bible passages 2

Passages (cont.)

Luke 23: 32–43 (The penitent thief)

Two other men, both criminals, were also led out with him to be executed. When they came to the place called the Skull, there they crucified him, along with the criminals – one on his right, the other on his left. Jesus said 'Father, forgive them, for they do not know what they are doing'. And they divided up his clothes by casting lots. The people stood watching, and the rulers even sneered at him. They said, 'He saved others; let him save himself if he is the Christ of God, the Chosen One.'

The soldiers also came up and mocked him. They offered him wine vinegar and said, 'If you are the king of the Jews, save yourself.'

There was a written notice above him, which read: THIS IS THE KING OF THE JEWS.

One of the criminals who hung there hurled insults at him: 'Aren't you the Christ? Save yourself and us!'

The other criminal rebuked him. 'Don't you fear God,' he said, 'since you are under the same sentence? We are punished justly, for we are getting what our deeds deserve. But this man has done nothing wrong.'

Then he said, 'Jesus, remember me when you come into your kingdom.'

Jesus answered him, 'I tell you the truth, today you will be with me in paradise.'

The thief realized and accepted he was being punished for his crime. He also knew that Jesus was innocent. Whether he understood that Jesus was the Messiah or God's son we are not told. What we are told is that the thief asked Jesus to remember him in heaven. Jesus promised him he would. Jesus forgave him. It is never too late to repent.

Matthew 18: 23–35 (The unmerciful servant)

The kingdom of heaven is like a king who wanted to settle accounts with his servants.

As he began the settlement, a man who owed him ten thousand talents was brought to him. Since he was not able to pay, the master ordered that he and his wife and his children and all that he had be sold to repay the debt. The servant fell on his knees before him. 'Be patient with me,' he begged, 'and I will pay back everything.' The servant's master took pity on him, cancelled the debt and let him go. But when that servant went out, he found one of his fellow-servants who owed him a hundred denarii. He grabbed him and began to choke him. 'Pay back what you owe me!' he demanded.

His fellow-servant fell to his knees and begged him, 'Be patient with me, and I will pay you back.' But he refused. Instead, he went off and had the man thrown into prison until he could pay the debt. When the other servants saw what had happened, they were greatly distressed and went and told their master everything that had happened. Then the master called the servant in. 'You wicked servant,' he said, 'I cancelled that debt of yours because you begged me to. Shouldn't you have had mercy on your fellow-servant just as I had on you?' In anger his master turned him over to the jailers to be tortured, until he should pay back all he owed. This is how my heavenly Father will treat each of you unless you forgive your brother from you heart.

The main meaning is two-fold. If we want to be forgiven by God and by others, then we must be prepared to forgive others, too, however 'small or big' the sin.

The king represents God who forgives our many sins, however great. The first servant is forgiven but he is not prepared to do the same for a lesser sin. God warns we will be punished for not forgiving. We must also let God do the punishing.

Philemon 1–25 (Justice and reconciliation)

Paul, a prisoner of Christ Jesus, and Timothy our brother, To Philemon our dear friend and fellow-worker,…:

Grace to you and peace from God our Father and the Lord Jesus Christ. I always thank my God as I remember you in my prayers, because I hear about your faith in the Lord Jesus and your love for all the saints. I pray that you may be active in sharing your faith, so that you will have a full understanding of every good thing we have in Christ. Your love has given me great joy and encouragement, because you, brother, have refreshed the hearts of the saints.

Therefore, although in Christ I could be bold and order you to do what you ought to do, yet I appeal to you on the basis of love. I then, as Paul – an old man and now also a prisoner of Christ Jesus – I appeal to you for my son Onesimus, who became my son while I was in chains. Formerly he was useless to you, but now he has become useful both to you and to me.

I am sending him – who is my very heart – back to you. I would have liked to keep him with me so that he could take your place in helping me while I am in chains for the gospel. But I did not want to do anything without your consent, so that any favour you do will be spontaneous and not forced. Perhaps the reason he was separated from you for a little while was that you might have him back for good – no longer as a slave, but better than a slave, as a dear brother. He is very dear to me but even dearer to you, both as a man and as a brother in the Lord. So if you consider me a partner, welcome him as you would welcome me. If he has done you any wrong or owes you anything, charge it to me.

I, Paul, am writing this with my own hand. I will pay it back – not to mention that you owe me your very self. I do wish, brother, that I may have some benefit from you in the Lord; refresh my heart in Christ. Confident of your obedience, I write to you, knowing that you will do even more than I ask. And one thing more: Prepare a guest room for me, because I hope to be restored to you in answer to your prayers.

Epaphras, my fellow-prisoner in Christ Jesus, sends you greetings. And so do Mark, Aristarchus, Demas and Luke, my fellow-workers. The grace of the Lord Jesus Christ be with your spirit.

This is a real life 'forgiving against the odds' story. Paul begins in a formal Roman letter writing style, addressing Philemon, a member of the early church. Philemon has money and can afford to buy slaves. Paul however writes to him as a fellow Christian.

Philemon had a slave called Onesimus who ran away. There was only one punishment – death. Paul has somehow befriended Onesimus, who is now like Paul's son. Christians today should do the same thing, befriending those in need.

Paul now asks Philemon to do something that would make the tongues start wagging – to take Onesimus back, to forgive him and to really mean it as a Christian. Paul says that in God's eyes, Onesimus is not a slave, he is a fellow brother. It will of course take courage to do this.

This is consistent with Jesus' teaching. Christians must be different from other 'good people' in behaviour, words and actions. It is easy to say 'I forgive you', but hard to put it into practice and mean it. In this case, Philemon will not have Onesimus put to death. Sadly, we are not told the outcome.

Activities

1   Reread Matthew 5: 38–48 (Teaching on forgiveness). Now try to explain why it is so difficult to put Jesus' words into action. **C 2.2**

2   Do you agree that revenge is 'a natural human reaction'? Give reasons. **PS 2.1**

3   Choose one parable from Jesus that is about forgiveness.
    a   Write it out briefly, including only the main points.
    b   Explain how it fits in with Jesus' teaching about forgiveness. **PS 2.1, 2.2**

4   Imagine you are the penitent thief on the cross. Write down your conversation with Jesus, including your thoughts and feelings. End with Jesus forgiving you. How do you feel now? **C 2.3**

Exam questions to practise

Below are some sample exam questions for paper 2B. To help you score full marks, the first three questions are followed by some tips from examiners. Before attempting the remaining two questions, try to work out your own strategy for approaching them.

1 Explain why Christians disagree over the issue of capital punishment. You must use at least one Bible passage. (6)

2 Look at the picture below, then answer the questions that follow it.

a What is the aim of punishment shown here? (1)

b What did Jesus teach to replace this attitude? (3)

c Explain one reason why it is difficult to put Jesus' words in to action? (2)

3 What can we learn about mercy and forgiveness from the parable of the unmerciful servant? (4)

Now try questions 4 and 5 on your own. Before you write your answers, spend some time thinking of your approach.

4 Explain why many Christians believe that reform is the most important aim of punishment. (5)

5 'Christians should always forgive.' Do you agree? Give reasons for your answer, showing you have considered more than one point of view. Refer to Christianity in your answer. (5)

How to score full marks

1 Think about views for and against capital punishment, which are Christian in nature. You must include at least one Bible passage.

2 Consider the following points.
    a Make sure it is an *aim*, not a type of punishment
    b Think about what Jesus said 'But I tell you …'.

    c You need to write down one reason, which will be worth one mark. Then you need to explain what it means, which is the second mark.

3 *Do not* rewrite the parable. You will gain few or no marks. Go through the main characters. How many are there? What do we learn from each person?

Prejudice and discrimination

This section includes:

- Prejudice and discrimination: an introduction
- Types of prejudice and discrimination
- Jesus and discrimination
- Nelson Mandela
- Archbishop Desmond Tutu
- Martin Luther King
- Bible passages 1
- Bible passages 2
- Exam questions to practise

Prejudice is the biased thought, discrimination the action. Some of the most horrific crimes are committed due to prejudice of some kind. Prejudice and the resulting discrimination are not just about race (racism) or colour. They can also be about gender, disability, religion, social class, which school you attended, sexual orientation, where you live – you name it, there will be prejudice.

This section will consider a variety of issues relating to prejudice and discrimination and Christian responses. It will also examine Bible teaching, and the lives of famous Christians who fought against discrimination.

Prejudice and discrimination: an introduction

Discrimination Prejudice in action. It is acting differently towards someone because of, for example, their colour, race, gender or disability.

Prejudice Pre-judging – that is, having a biased feeling or attitude about a person or a group of people before you know the facts.

The law

In the UK, **discrimination** has been made illegal by a number of Acts of Parliament (see below). However, it is easy to legislate against discrimination, but another matter to change deep-rooted **prejudices** and to prove discrimination.

- The *Race Relations Act 1976* made it illegal to discriminate on the grounds of colour, race or nationality in the areas of employment, housing, education, providing goods, services and facilities. It was needed because ethnic groups were often segregated, and landlords and employers often specified, for example, 'no Asians'. The aim of this act was integration, so that people of different races could live side by side, but keep

their own cultures. The Commission for Racial Equality (CRE) was set up to deal with cases of discrimination.

- The *Amendment Act (Race Relations) 2000* was introduced with the intention of strengthening the 1976 act, not replacing it. The main thrust of the new act targeted the public sector – hospitals, schools, public councils and government ministers – in four areas. Their new standards would influence the private sector.

1. It extended protection against racial discrimination by public authorities and placed on them a new enforceable positive duty.

2. Chief Officers of the police would now be liable for acts of discrimination by officers under their control.

3. It prohibited discrimination by government ministers or departments in the appointment and approval of public officers, including conferring honours or peerages in the House of Lords.

4. It limited the circumstances in which 'safeguarding national security' could be used to justify discrimination.

Family – this will be the first source of ideas, and includes a child's relatives and main carer if parents are working; by the age of five prejudices will be fact

Scapegoating – when a minority group is blamed for all the economic ills

Media – children learn ideas especially from television, for example, cartoon heroines are nearly always big busted with pencil-thin waists, and at one time in police dramas the drug dealers always came from Liverpool

Peer group – some children alter their ideas to fit in with those of their friends and develop similar attitudes

Where does prejudice come from?

Patriotism – some people call themselves patriotic; the more extreme want to get rid of ethnic minorities and instil hatred

Fear – in time of economic downturn minority groups will be blamed and other groups fear they will take over

Ignorance – it is often easier to believe a rumour than to check out the real facts

- The *Equal Pay Act 1975* stated that women were to be paid the same as men if doing the same (or a broadly similar) job. Criteria were written down to work out equivalent jobs.

- The *Sex Discrimination Act 1975* meant that it became illegal for an employer to advertise specifically that men or women were required for a job. There were some exceptions, such as men only priests in some churches. Also, the Act stated that all girls had the same right as boys for a free education until the age of sixteen. Women who took maternity leave had to have the same opportunities as men for promotion. A further act made it possible for a woman's pension to go to her husband if she died before him.

- Although much had already been done for people with disabilities (particularly those registered as disabled), the *Disability Discrimination Act 1995* aimed to help those with lesser disabilities. Disability is defined in this act as anyone who has a physical or mental impairment which has a substantial and long-term effect on his or her ability to carry out normal day-to-day activities. You do not have to be registered disabled to qualify.

The declared intentions of the act were to give disabled people new rights in employment, obtaining goods and services, buying or renting any type of property, transport and education. A council was set up to advise the government on disability discrimination issues. The act is still being phased in. This is because alterations can take time – for example, raising money, planning, building and finding the money. Some employers warned of bankruptcy if the changes were implemented too quickly. Churches and church halls are not exempt from this ruling, and must make alterations to include ramps, new toilets and new seating.

In 1999 'Information provision' became law. This meant that information from agencies providing any kind of service should have it available in Braille or on audiotape. (An example is a bus timetable.)

It is hoped by blind people that discrimination against guide dogs will also be covered – for example, taxis must now carry guide dogs free of charge.

Even guide dogs for the blind sometimes suffer discrimination.

Activity

Using the Internet, look up one of the acts on pages 62–3. Then answer the following questions:

a Why was it necessary to have such an act?

b What did it set out to do?

c Has it been successful in its aims?

A good place to start your research is with the following sites:

- www.humanrights.gov.au/sex_discrimination/know/

- www.humanrights.gov.au/sex_discrimination/know/ **IT 2.3**

Key points

- Children are influenced from birth and learn prejudices before they even reach school.

- Two of the biggest causes of prejudice are fear and ignorance of someone you have never met.

- There have been several Acts of Parliament that address discrimination.

Types of prejudice and discrimination

There are many different types of prejudice and discrimination.

- *Racism* is discrimination against someone because of his or her race. People are defined according to their race (ethnic group). In the past, people, such as the police on arrest, classified the person. More recently, the person concerned will classify his or her own race.

Below is the list of categories found on many forms.

White	British
	Irish
	any other white
Mixed	white and black Caribbean
	white and black African
	white and black Asian
	any other mix
Asian/Asian British	Indian
	Pakistani
	Bangladeshi
	any others
Black/Black British	Caribbean
	African
	any others
Chinese	
Other ethnic group	

- *Colour discrimination* is treating someone differently because of the colour of his or her skin.
- *Religious discrimination* is treating someone differently because of his or her religion. Some times it depends on which **denomination** these people belong to.
- *Disability discrimination* is treating someone differently because he or she is disabled in some way.
- *Gender discrimination* is treating someone differently because of his or her sex (gender) – that is, whether male or female. It is also called **sexism**.

Examples of discrimination

- *Example of racism*. A man who is Asian British is told by a landlord that the room he would like to rent is taken – even though it is not. The landlord is prejudiced as he does not like Asians, and he put this prejudice into action.

  The Metropolitan Police have been accused on 'institutional racism'. Figures in January 2001 showed that black people are still five times more likely than whites to be stopped, searched and arrested.

- *Example of colour discrimination*. An African British boy whose great-grandparents live in Nigeria is told by his PE teacher and two boys that he should have been able to run quicker than he did (and win) as black people have the advantage of being able to run fast.

  The most extreme form of racism and colour discrimination was apartheid in South Africa (see pages 70–3).

- *Examples of disability discrimination*. People who are regarded as disabled are often treated differently. An adult in a wheelchair who lives an independent life with his wife and children often finds he cannot gain access to buildings and kerbs are too high. Someone else has to go with him. If he wants to go to the cinema, he finds numbers of disabled people are limited – he is a fire hazard!

Is it fair that you should be discriminated against simply because of your race?

How would you feel if you were considered a fire hazard?

A deaf girl at school finds people shout at her. The majority of people are unable to use sign language. It is fine with teachers who know she is deaf, but if someone does not know she is deaf she is shouted at for not paying attention or not writing down what to do.

- *Example of gender (sex) discrimination*. A well-qualified woman applies for a job at an insurance company. Although she is the best person for the job, she is not offered it. The owner is male and it is his belief that women should be at home with the children. He thinks that working women are not reliable because they might need extra time off to care for their children when they are ill.

At the end of 2000 women were still earning, on average, twenty per cent less than their male colleagues.

Results of prejudice and discrimination

- Prejudice leads to discrimination, because most people act on their thoughts.
- People are attacked on purpose and sometimes the attack ends in murder. The number of race crimes in England and Wales was 48,000 in 2000. For example, in April and May 2001 there was serious trouble in Oldham, with rioting by both Asian and white communities.

- Some people, including children, are driven to suicide.
- Rumours become fact.
- One tragic result is genocide, when someone decides to murder a whole race (for example, Hitler had six million Jews killed).

Church of England policy

In 1985, a major report was published by the Anglican Synod called 'Faith in the City'. It concluded that racial discrimination was still a challenge to be overcome in society. The authors said Christians should make a first move by complying with existing laws against racism.

Activities

1 Using the Internet, newspapers and magazines, find examples of racism, sexism, colour and disability discrimination. Read the articles in groups/class and discuss the following questions.
  a How did the discrimination affect those concerned?
  b Has anything been done as a result (for example, an enquiry)? **C 2.1a, IT 2.1**
2 Which kind of discrimination do you think is the worst, if any? List your reasons. **PS 2.1**
3 Try to explain what is meant by the term 'positive discrimination'. **P 2.1, 2.2**

Key points

- Prejudice is the thought, discrimination is the action.
- There are many types of discrimination, not just racism.
- The results of prejudice and discrimination are always going to hurt someone and at its worst can cause war or death.

Jesus and discrimination

Key terms

Lepers People who were made total outcasts because they had a skin disease which was thought to be highly contagious. They lived with other lepers in colonies. They were not allowed to go near other people. Food was left for them, rather than handed to them.

Sometimes it can be very hard to overcome prejudice and deal with real people in real situations. Here are some examples:

- What would you do if you disliked **homosexuals**? You get a good job, good pay and conditions, and good chances of promotion. Then you find out the owner of the company – who you will have to get on with – is homosexual and lives with his partner.

- What would you do if you disliked people who are not the same colour as you? For instance, you get very friendly with a boy or girl by chatting on the Internet. You know you live quite close. You share a joke, a laugh, then agree to meet up. At that meeting, it turns out the person is a different colour to you. What do you do?

Jesus and race

In Luke 7: 1–10 (The centurion's servant) – see page 78 – the centurion, who was Roman, recognized the greatness of Jesus, who was prepared to come and heal his servant.

The centurion realized that Jesus would be regarded as 'unclean' if he entered a gentile (non-Jewish) house. He believed that Jesus was perfectly able to heal the servant from where he was. Jesus responded by healing the servant from a distance and saying, 'I have not found such great faith even in Israel.' Jesus praised the simple faith of a gentile, another race of people.

Jesus and religion

The Samaritans were hated by the Jews and vice versa. Jews regarded Samaritans as having corrupted the Jewish religion by marrying local people.

Jesus deliberately chose a Samaritan as the hero of his parable of the good Samaritan (Luke 10: 25–37 – see page 76) to demonstrate who our neighbours are. The listeners would have expected the Samaritan to kill the wounded man. You can almost imagine the gasps of horror when Jesus finished the story!

Jesus has a point – it is easy to help someone you do not know if they are the same religion or race as you. It is when you have to face up to your prejudices that the going gets tough.

AIDs cannot be caught by being close to an infected person.

Jesus and disability

At the time of Jesus, the accepted belief in most societies was that if you became ill and disabled you were being punished by God for sin. If you were born disabled, then your parents were being punished for some great sin. That was why Jesus forgave people their sins when he healed them.

Jesus was not afraid of disability and disease. He felt compassion and healed people who suffered from these. When he healed **lepers**, Jesus not only spoke to them, but also he touched them, which was unheard of, making himself unclean according to Jewish law. The modern-day equivalent was when Princess Diana visited AIDS patients and sat holding their hands and then hugged them.

When Jesus healed blind people, he let them feel his hands and face first and he told them what he was doing. With deaf people he often wrote for them using a stick in the sand. Similarly, when he healed Jairus' daughter (Luke 8: 40–2, 49–56), he held her hands then asked that she be given something to eat. He was not in the least bit put off by illness and disability – if the person had faith, Jesus healed. He showed understanding of their disability, such as letting the blind touch him.

Jesus and gender

In the time of Jesus, it was not considered right for men to speak to women unless they were related – and even then, it was within the privacy of the home.

Women were expected to care for the children. Unmarried women or wives who could not have children were pitied or scorned. This did not bother Jesus. He healed men and women. He spoke to a Samaritan woman and ended up changing her life (John 4: 5–10, 27–30).

Two of his best friends were Martha and Mary, sisters of Lazarus. Jesus often went to their home it seems to find peace and quiet (a 'bolt hole'). He let the sisters listen to him, not just allow them to serve him.

When Jesus was in Simon the Pharisee's house, a woman poured perfume on his feet (Mark 14: 3–9). She was told off, as etiquette dictated that women did not go near men unless invited. Jesus had let a woman, unrelated to him, come close and touch his feet. He was breaking convention.

When Jesus was crucified, the women followers gathered round. And when he rose on Easter Day it was to women that Jesus first appeared.

Activities

1 Pages 66 and 67 have given examples of Jesus dealing with people. From the evidence on these pages, do you think Jesus was ever prejudiced? Give reasons for your answer. **PS 2.1, 2.2**

2 Imagine you are either a leper or Jairus' daughter. Write a letter to a friend explaining what happened. Include your feelings and what you think about Jesus. **C 2.2, 2.3**

3 What could local churches do to cater for the disabled? If you are visiting a church, you could look for evidence of this. **PS 2.1, 2.2**

Key points

- Jesus dealt with all types of people, from high ranking to the lowest.
- Jesus disregarded tradition or etiquette if it interfered with his ministry.
- Jesus understood the needs of many different groups of people.

Christian attitudes to women in Britain

The debate about women priests is almost as contentious as that surrounding abortion. Some denominations accept them fully, some accept them partially and some do not accept them at all. The United Reformed Church accepts women priests totally, the Anglican church differs from area to area and the Roman Catholic Church does not allow women priests.

The Roman Catholic Church

Women are still forbidden to be ordained in the Roman Catholic Church. Priests will argue a series of reasons why not. It is also said that women can become nuns if they wish to serve God or they can be lay workers using their skills.

The Anglican Church

By 1998, the Anglican Church ordained women fully as priests except in some male-only areas in parts of Asia and Africa. In some parishes in England, the church council decided that they would not accept a female priest.

Some male priests threatened to leave the Anglican Church in response and become Roman Catholic. In reality, some male priests did leave, but if they were married they could not become full Roman Catholic priests. However, over time, despite some vehement rejection of women priests, the issue has died down and most people now accept women priests are here to stay.

Arguments for and against women priests

Against

- From the earliest times it has been practice not to ordain women to the priesthood, thus it is tradition.
- The ministries of women mentioned in the New Testament had nothing to do with the sacraments (consecrating Holy Communion).
- The church fathers rejected women priests in every debate.
- Medieval church law again excluded women priests.
- In the Mass, the priest takes on the role of Christ which a woman cannot.
- Jesus chose twelve special male disciples and commissioned them to go out into the world, but no female ones.
- Paul taught that women should be silent in church (1 Corinthians 14: 34–5), and should not teach men (1 Timothy 2: 12).

Counter arguments

- Tradition was based on prejudice against women, regarded as inferior and unclean.
- Mary has perceived priestly function, in that she intercedes on our behalf with Jesus. Priscilla (Acts 18: 26) and Phoebe (Romans 16: 1) are mentioned in terms of a teaching ministry and leadership.
- The church fathers were prejudiced before the debate began.
- Medieval church law was based on the law of the founders and thus incorporated prejudices.
- The priest is re-enacting the Last Supper. When Jesus said, 'Do this to remember me', he did not say, 'Only men may take communion because I only had twelve male disciples with me'.
- Paul was known for his dislike of women and his ideas applied to how women were regarded in his society.

Women priests: the right or wrong thing to do?

The website www.womenpriests.org/ is devoted to women priests and it gives some extra reasons why women should become priests:

- In baptism women and men share equally in the death and resurrection of Jesus. The Holy Spirit descends on men *and* women.

- The male-only attitude is part of a set of derogatory values about women (regarding sex and body).

- It is recorded that until the ninth century AD the church ordained women to become full deacons.

- There is a devotion to Mary as priest; in Mary the ban against women has already been overcome.

- Other denominations have studied and prayed and they now ordain women as priests. This must be the mind of Christ.

Comments from men about women priests

'Women priests distract me.'

'Women are suited to the ministry just as men are, you get good and bad vicars whether male or female.'

'I will not receive Holy Communion from a woman.'

'I thought at first I would hate a woman vicar, but in my last church there was one and she was the best thing that ever happened to that church.'

Comments from women about women priests

'Women vicars would be better with young children.'

'I prefer a male vicar, but if a woman was all that was available I would be OK about it.'

'I think they'd be sympathetic to people with problems, or who are sick or bereaved.'

'I hate women priests wearing a shirt and clerical collar, imitating men. They should design their own.'

Activities

1 Find out which denominations allow women priests and which do not. **PS 1.1**

2 What are your opinions about women priests? **P 1.1**

3 Do you think the church can claim to not be prejudiced when women priests are not allowed? Give reasons for your answer. **PS 2.1, 2.2**

Key points

- The issue of women priests has been hotly debated.

- Women can become priests or ministers in most denominations.

- Women may not become priests in the Roman Catholic Church.

Nelson Mandela

During the twentieth century, many Christians worked against the many different forms of prejudice and discrimination. Three Christians who have worked against racism are Nelson Mandela, Archbishop Desmond Tutu and Martin Luther King. In the next few pages, we will look at each of these people.

Influences on Mandela

In South Africa there was a system in place called **apartheid**. This meant that people were separated according to colour. Black people came off worst. They had no rights, no vote, no proper jobs, bad housing on the worst land and no running water.

Black people had to carry passes, were often imprisoned and were kept separate from whites in everything. Even park benches were labelled for white or black use.

The ANC

The **ANC (African National Congress)** was founded to fight for black rights. The proportions of people living in South Africa were as shown in the pie chart opposite.

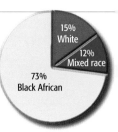

15% White

12% Mixed race

73% Black African

Mandela joined the ANC in 1944 and tried to set up talks with the government. He was totally convinced that apartheid was wrong and that the Bible supported his view. Mandela battled within his mind, but decided there was no option other than to use terrorism. This was a necessary evil to defeat a greater evil. In 1963, Mandela and several of his friends were arrested, charged with trying to overthrow the government and sentenced to life imprisonment.

Nelson Mandela

'I have cherished the ideal of a free society in which all persons live together in harmony and equal opportunities. It is an ideal which I hope to live for, but if need be, it is an ideal for which I am prepared to die.'

1918	Born in South Africa. Grew up as a devout Methodist. Trained as a black lawyer in Johannesburg.
1944	Joined the ANC and tried to negotiate in the name of Christ's peace.
1963	Was sentenced to life imprisonment on Robben Island. Continued his campaign in prison and worked to help his fellow prisoners.
1980s	Worldwide campaign to end apartheid and free Mandela.
February 1990	Mandela was freed.
June 1999	Retired.
Other details	After a conscience battle he had decided that violence was a necessary evil.

Freedom

The years 1983 and 1984 saw headlines calling for Mandela's freedom. In 1985, President Botha said Mandela would be set free if he gave up his campaign and lived in a remote area. This was declined. Few countries would trade with South Africa and their sporting teams, and athletes were banned from international events.

In 1989, President Frederick Willem de Klerk came to power and in 1990 he declared that the ANC and other banned groups were now legal. He called for talks to work out a new constitution. On 11 February 1990, Mandela was set free after 27 years. In 1994, there were free elections and Mandela became the first democratically elected president of South Africa.

Problems

Mandela began the slow process of healing wounds, teaching people to forgive and to work together. His aim was to redistribute wealth. He had to start from scratch, building multi-racial schools for all races and beginning to reclaim areas from white people. He nationalized key functions (brought them under government control), such as the electricity supply.

At the beginning of the twenty-first century, South Africa is still faced with enormous inequalities and people want things done quicker. One thing Mandela did achieve was his tremendous public relations job. He visited boycotting countries and persuaded them to trade, invest or work in South Africa.

Many books have been written about Mandela. He wrote his autobiography called *Long Walk to Freedom*.

Extracts from Mandela's autobiography

The dark years
Time may stand still for those of us in prison but it did not halt for those outside. I was reminded of this when I was visited by my mother in the spring of 1968 … my mother suddenly seemed very old … My mother had lost a great deal of weight, her face appeared haggard. …

I looked back and evaluated my own life. Her difficulties, her poverty made me question whether I had taken the right path – had I put the people's welfare before that of my own family?

Freedom
On the evening of May 2 Mr de Klerk made a concession speech – after more than 300 years the white minority was conceding defeat and turning over power to the black majority. I went on stage about nine o'clock. Mrs King, wife of Martin Luther King, was on the podium that night as I said: 'This is one of the most important moments in the life of our country. Now with joy we can loudly proclaim "Free at last!" I stand before you humbled by your courage … I am your servant … This is a time to heal the old wounds and build a new South Africa.'

Activities

1   List the reasons that made Nelson Mandela work against apartheid. **C 1.2**

2   What has Mandela achieved? **PS 2.1**

3   Read the extracts from Mandela's book then answer the questions below:
    a   Do you think he made the right decision to help his people at the expense of his mother? Give reasons.
    b   What points was he making in his freedom speech? **PS 2.1, C 2.2**

Key points

- His dilemma was whether he should use terrorism or not. Mandela and his supporters would argue that his choice of violence was the right one to make.
- Problems still remain in South Africa – there are old wounds to be healed and huge inequalities to be sorted.

Archbishop Desmond Tutu

Archbishop Desmond Tutu

'My vision is of a South Africa that is totally non-racial. A new South Africa, a free South Africa, where all of us, black and white together, will walk tall, will hold hands as we stride forth ... to usher in the new South Africa where people will matter because they are human beings made in the image of God.'

1931	Born in South Africa. Educated in the inferior education system for black children. Trained as a vicar after gaining his teaching diploma.
1961	Ordained as priest.
1962–65	Studied in the UK. Lectured in South African universities.
1976	Became Bishop of Lesotho, worked for peace.
1984	Won Nobel Peace Prize.
1985	Became Bishop of Johannesburg.
1986	Became Archbishop of Cape Town – used his position to campaign against apartheid.
Other details	Always advocated non-violence.

Influences on Tutu

As a black child Tutu struggled to gain an adequate education. This influenced his anti-apartheid stance in later life. After studying he became a priest in 1961 – first working in London, then lecturing throughout South Africa.

Tutu preached against apartheid. When told that he should keep out of politics by the police and some fellow priests he responded: 'I am puzzled as to which Bible people are using when they suggest that religion and politics do not mix.'

Dilemma

Tutu faced a dilemma: he opposed apartheid but apartheid was state supported by the army and the police. If you denounced apartheid you were branded a terrorist or a communist, risking torture, imprisonment or death. He questioned whether to fight with violence or non-violence.

In 1976, he became bishop of Lesotho, gaining some authority; by which time he had chosen to lead the non-violent struggle using marches, boycotts, petitions and drawing attention to his actions by inviting the world's media to events. For example, the BBC filmed state police attacking unarmed children.

Nobel Peace Prize

In 1984, Archbishop Tutu gained the Nobel Peace Prize. In his speech he said: 'I will not be told by secular authorities what gospel I must preach!'

In 1985, he was Bishop of Johannesburg, which gave him a new platform. 'Christians must test government policies against Christian teaching.' He again and again denounced apartheid as one of the 'most vicious systems since Nazism; the day I am proved wrong I will burn my Bible, the source of all teaching.'

Tutu received the Nobel Peace Prize.

Mandela chose him to lead South Africa's Truth and Reconciliation Commission – a group of men and women chosen to investigate crimes committed by *all* sides during apartheid. Tutu was not afraid of delving deep, even into atrocities committed by black people. He was appalled at the evil uncovered on all sides, but believed it was necessary to try and heal a traumatized, wounded people.

Desmond Tutu is extremely ill, at the moment. He is dying of cancer, but nurses say he never complains.

LEARN from the PAST; LIVE in the PRESENT; PLAN for the FUTURE!!!

Archbishop

Becoming the first black Anglican Archbishop of Cape Town in 1986 gave Desmond Tutu even more power, yet he remained humble. His personality radiates God's love and even the most hardened soldier finds it hard to remain unmoved. His opposition to apartheid stems from his simple faith. He is a man who studies his Bible daily, prays and worships God.

Archbishop Tutu always opposed violence. He said: 'If you use violence I will find it difficult to speak for the cause of liberation. You cannot use methods that our enemy will use against us.'

End of apartheid

Archbishop Tutu's work did not stop with the end of apartheid. He continues to speak out against injustice. He is called 'the voice of the forgotten' – that is, the poorest people, children and other minorities. He wrote a book called *Voice of one crying in the Wilderness*, in which he spoke for social justice, encouraging others to take action: 'What we need is an upsurge of international courage, moral indignation and human solidarity to demand action …'

Activities

1 List the reasons why you think it took so long to end apartheid, despite the use of violence and non-violence. **C 1.2**

2 Make a note of what you consider to be the biggest factor in ending apartheid. A good place to start your research is with http://news.bbc.co.uk **IT 2.1, PS 2.1**

3 List the problems that still remain in South Africa. Why do you think they have not yet been solved? **PS 2.1, 2.2**

Key points

- Archbishop Desmond Tutu is seen as the opposite of Nelson Mandela, although they are both Christians.
- Mandela decided that violence was needed. Tutu chose non-violence, preaching a gospel of reconciliation.
- Tutu's belief in God kept him going. He believed the Bible taught him all he needed to know!

Martin Luther King

Martin Luther King

'I have a dream that one day this nation will rise up and live out the true meaning of its creed. We hold these truths to be self-evident that all men are created equal. I have a dream that my four little children will one day live in a nation where they will not be judged by the colour of their skin but by the content of their character.'

1929	Born in Georgia USA. Well educated for a black child.
1948	Ordained a pastor of Baptist Church.
1955	Bus Boycott began his active campaign against racism.
1961	Led series of sit-ins and rallies, which gained coverage throughout the USA.
1964	Achieved Civil Rights Act, some segregation ended.
1965	Voting Rights Act, black people had same voting rights as whites.
4 April 1968	Murdered by James Earl Ray, who claimed he'd been set up.
Other details	King always advocated non-violent protest – 'meet hate with love'.

Influences on King

When Martin Luther King was born in 1929, the USA, especially in the South, followed a policy of **segregation** against black people including separate schools, transport systems and churches.

The 1950s

During his studies, Martin Luther King became influenced by the great Indian leader Mahatma Gandhi and his writings on non-violence. King started to speak out against segregation and the oppression of black people, and became involved with the Bus **Boycott** in Montgomery. This was in 1955, when black people stopped using buses until they were treated equally. King insisted that there be no violent revenge, 'meeting hate with love'.

In 1957 King continued to preach non-violent direct action including marches, boycotts and sit-ins. More white people joined his campaign.

The 1960s

In the early 1960s Martin Luther King led demonstrations against segregated housing, hotels, restaurants and transport. Many white businesses never recovered from the loss of trade.

In 1963, King organized a march of hundreds of school children aged up to sixteen years, in downtown Birmingham (USA), to protest against inferior schooling for black children. They were singing and chanting, waving home-made banners. King invited the world's press. The police commissioner sent police with attack dogs and water hoses to end the march. Scenes of children being attacked by dogs and being knocked down by pressure hoses were shown on TV and in newspapers worldwide.

State police set dogs on unarmed civilians.

The Ku Klux Klan held secret meetings where they tortured and often killed black people.

He wrote an important document which argued that individuals had the moral right and responsibility to disobey unjust laws. He felt his Christian beliefs spurred him on. He believed he was adding to what Paul wrote in Romans 13: 1 about obeying the state, bringing it up to date and clarifying points.

In 1965, King campaigned for equal voting rights. A peaceful march was broken up by police using tear gas and beatings. Again King made sure it was televized. In the same year, the Voting Rights Act ended the use of the special reading test and other tests that had prevented black people from voting.

Violence erupts

By the mid-1960s young blacks began to question King's abhorrence of violence. The Black Power group formed and looked to the philosophy of Malcolm X, a black Muslim leader who argued for the rights of black people to use violence against attack. The Ku Klux Klan – a secret terrorist group who hated black people and often burned them alive – counter-attacked.

Assassination

Martin Luther King was murdered by James Earl Ray on 4 August 1968. King's importance grew worldwide. Indeed, he once said: 'When I die my work will only just be beginning.' The third Monday

Jesse Jackson: he might not be in a position of power had it not been for the work of Martin Luther King.

in January is now a national holiday in honour and memory of King. More and more black people campaigned for rights and won them. Black people have risen to power, such as the black Mayor of New York, and Jesse Jackson, who stood for president.

Activities

1 Do you think it was right of King to continue his campaign despite the danger to his wife and family? Give reasons for your answer. **C 2.1a**

2 Read the quote below:

> We can only see with open eyes;
> We can only listen with open ears;
> We can only think with open minds.

   a Explain what you think is meant by 'open eyes', 'open ears' and 'open minds'.

   b List how you feel this fits with King's character. **PS 2.1, 2.2**

3 Imagine you are a British television reporter covering one of King's marches, boycotts or sit-ins for the BBC. You witness the dramatic events of peaceful protesters being attacked. Choose the name and date of incident (for example, the children's march). Write your exclusive report, which includes interviews with Christian pastors and King himself. Video your report for the BBC news. **C 2.1b**

Key points

● King felt led by God to use his public speaking skills and charismatic personality to lead campaigns against racism.

● In all areas King chose non-violent action. His motto was to meet hate with love.

● Most of his achievements probably happened after his death, when it became more acceptable for black people to take public office.

Here you will find the relevant Bible passages that you will need for the prejudice and discrimination section. The passages are written out, then there is an explanation of what they mean.

Luke 10: 25–37 (The good Samaritan)

On one occasion an expert in the law stood up to test Jesus. 'Teacher,' he asked, 'what must I do to inherit eternal life?'

'What is written in the Law?' [Jesus] replied. 'How do you read it?'

He answered: '"Love the Lord your God with all your heart and with all your soul and with all your strength and with all your mind"; and, "Love your neighbour love yourself".'

'You have answered correctly,' Jesus replied. 'Do this and you will live.' But he wanted to justify himself, so he asked Jesus, 'And who is my neighbour?'

In reply Jesus said: 'A man was going down from Jerusalem to Jericho, when he fell into the hands of robbers. They stripped him of his clothes, beat him and went away, leaving him half-dead. A priest happened to be going down the same road, and when he saw the man, he passed by on the other side. So too, a Levite, when he came to the place and saw him, passed by on the other side. But a Samaritan, as he travelled, came where the man was; and when he saw him, he took pity on him. He went to him and bandaged his wounds, pouring on oil and wine. Then he put the man on his own donkey, brought him to an inn and took care of him. The next day he took out two silver coins and gave them to the innkeeper. "Look after him," he said, "and when I return, I will reimburse you for any extra expense you may have." Which of these three do you think was a neighbour to the man who fell into the hands of robbers?'

The expert in the law replied, 'The one who had mercy on him.'

Jesus told him, 'Go and do likewise.'

Jesus told this story in response to the question 'Who is my neighbour?' As the story developed listeners would have changed their attitude.

The Jewish man was attacked and the crowd would have little sympathy, thinking 'stupid man, going on his own along a notorious route'.

When the priest came along they expected him to help. But he walked on. The excuse might have been he would have become technically unclean if he touched the man, then there would be a long ritual to get clean so he could work in the temple again.

The crowd would have expected the Levite to help – they were godly helpers in the temple. His excuse might have been he would be late for temple duties or the same as the priest.

When the Samaritan came along, the crowd expected murder! The Jews and Samaritans were such enemies that they expected the Samaritan to take the chance to finish him off. You can imagine the gasps as he helps the Jewish man, takes him to an inn and then pays for the week. Who is my neighbour? Anyone who is in need, regardless of race, colour, religion, even your enemy!

Galatians 3: 28 (All one in Christ)

There is neither Jew nor Greek, slave nor free, male nor female, for you are all one in Christ Jesus.

Paul points out that in God's eyes we are all equal. Some people say that this passage is against slavery. It does not mention Paul's society, but it does say that God does not put one person above another. This links in with other passages of Paul's, such as his idea of the church as a body made up of different parts, Christ as the head and all the parts of equal importance.

Acts 11: 1–18 (Peter and Cornelius)

The apostles and the brothers throughout Judea heard that the Gentiles also had received the word of God. So when Peter went up to Jerusalem, the circumcized believers criticized him and said, 'You went into the house of uncircumcized men and ate with them.'

Peter began and explained everything to them precisely as it had happened: 'I was in the city of Joppa praying, and in a trance I saw a vision. I saw something like a large sheet being let down from heaven by its four corners, and it came down to where I was. I looked into it and saw four-footed animals of the earth, wild beasts, reptiles, and birds of the air. Then I heard a voice telling me, "Get up, Peter. Kill and eat." I replied, "Surely not, Lord! Nothing impure or unclean has ever entered my mouth." The voice spoke from heaven a second time, "Do not call anything impure that God has made clean." This happened three times, and then it was pulled up to heaven again. Right then three men who had been sent to me from Caesarea stopped at the house where I was staying. The Spirit told me to have no hesitation about going with them. These six brothers also went with me, and we entered the man's house. He told us how he had seen an angel appear in his house and say, "Send to Joppa for Simon who is called Peter. He will bring you a message through which you and all your household will be saved." As I began to speak, the Holy Spirit came on them as he had come on us at the beginning. Then I remembered what the Lord had said: "John baptized with water, but you will be baptized with the Holy Spirit". So if God gave them the same gift as he gave us, who believed in the Lord Jesus Christ, who was I to think that I could oppose God?'

When they heard this, they had no further objections and praised God, saying, 'So then, God has granted even the Gentiles repentance unto life.'

Peter recounts how his set prejudices were challenged by God. Peter dreamt about Jewish food laws – kosher and non-kosher food – all mixed up together. Peter was horrified, as all the kosher food was now regarded as unclean, as it had mixed with non-kosher food such as pork. On three occasions Peter was told to eat. God said that he had made everything and made them clean. Peter woke and men sent by Cornelius arrived.

Peter later explained that if he had not had the dream, he would probably not have gone – he would become unclean on entering a gentile home. That apart, Peter would not have thought that the gospel was for gentiles on the whole. But this clearly showed Peter that the gospel is for gentiles too, and God has made them clean. No longer would these rituals keep people from knowing about God's kingdom.

Activity

What can Christians learn about dealing with people of other races or religions from the parable of the good Samaritan? Make a list.

PS 2.1, 2.2

Bible passages 2

Passages (cont.)

Luke 7: 1–10 (The centurion's servant)

When Jesus had finished saying all this in the hearing of the people, he entered Capernaum. There a centurion's servant, whom his master valued highly, was sick and about to die. The centurion heard of Jesus and sent some elders of the Jews to him, asking him to come and heal his servant. When they came to Jesus, they pleaded earnestly with him, 'This man deserves to have you do this, because he loves our nation and has built our synagogue.' So Jesus went with them.

He was not far from the house when the centurion sent friends to say to him: 'Lord, don't trouble yourself, for I do not deserve to have you come under my roof. That is why I did not even consider myself worthy to come to you. But say the word, and my servant will be healed. For I myself am a man under authority, with soldiers under me. I tell this one, "Go," and he goes; and that one, "Come," and he comes. I say to my servant, "Do this," and he does it.' When Jesus heard this, he was amazed at him, and turning to the crowd following him, he said, 'I tell you, I have not found such great faith even in Israel.' Then the men who had been sent returned to the house and found the servant well.

The centurion was Roman and well liked. For Jesus to go into his house would render Jesus unclean. This did not matter to Jesus, but the centurion showed respect for the other's religion. At some stage he had taken the trouble to learn about Judaism. He recognized in Jesus an authoritative person and said if he issued a command it would be done. He saw in Jesus someone who was greater than he. Jesus healed the servant. The key phrase here is 'I tell you, I have not found such great faith even in Israel.'

Notice too we are not told if the servant was Jewish or not. We are not told anything about the servant's origins at all (we are certainly not told if he was black). It is likely the servant was Jewish as he is described as a servant, not a slave.

What is important is that the centurion showed great faith and believed Jesus could help his servant. He also showed respect for another's religion and had found out some of the important customs. Additionally, he saw in Jesus a person superior to him.

Deuteronomy 24: 14–15, 17, 19, 21–2

Do not take advantage of a hired man who is poor and needy, whether he is a brother Israelite or an alien [foreigner] living in one of your towns. Pay him his wages each day before sunset, because he is poor and counting on it. (14–15)

Do not deprive the alien or the fatherless of justice, or take the cloak of the widow as a pledge. (17)

When you are harvesting in your field and you overlook a sheaf, do not go back to get it. Leave it for the alien, the fatherless and the widow, so that the Lord your God may bless you in all the work of your hands. (19)

When you harvest the grapes in your vineyard, do not go over the vines again. Leave what remains for the alien, the fatherless and the widow. Remember that you were slaves in Egypt. That is why I command you to do this. (21–2)

God gives the Jewish people strict instructions about the care of foreigners (some translations say 'aliens'). When the harvest is over, the poor and the foreigners are to be allowed to gather the leftovers. Wages too should be paid on time. God reminds his people of the time when they were persecuted in Egypt.

Leviticus 19: 33–4

'When an alien [foreigner] lives with you in your land, do not ill-treat him. The alien living with you must be treated as one of your native-born. Love him as yourself, for you were aliens in Egypt.'

Again, foreigners are to be well-treated because the Jews were once ill-treated in Egypt.

Amos 8: 3–7

'In that day,' declares the Sovereign Lord, 'the songs in the temple will turn to wailing. Many, many bodies – flung everywhere! Silence!'

Hear this, you who trample the needy and do away with the poor of the land, saying, 'When will the New Moon be over that we may sell grain, and the Sabbath be ended that we may market wheat?' – skimping the measure, boosting the price and cheating with dishonest scales, buying the poor with silver and the needy for a pair of sandals, selling even the sweepings with the wheat. The Lord has sworn by the Pride of Jacob: 'I will never forget anything they have done.'

God is furious that people cheat on the poor and foreigners by using false scales and adding sweepings to the wheat. It is all listed here and God hates it.

James 2: 1–9

My brothers, as believers in our glorious Lord Jesus Christ, don't show favouritism. Suppose a man comes into your meeting wearing a gold ring and fine clothes, and a poor man in shabby clothes also comes in. If you show special attention to the man wearing fine clothes and say, 'Here's a good seat for you,' but say to the poor man, 'You stand there' or 'Sit on the floor by my feet,' have you not discriminated among yourselves and become judges with evil thoughts?

Listen, my dear brothers: Has not God chosen those who are poor in the eyes of the world to be rich in faith and to inherit the kingdom he promised to those who love him? But you have insulted the poor. Is it not the rich who are exploiting you? Are they not the ones who are dragging you into court? Are they not the ones slandering the noble name of him to whom you belong?

If you really keep the royal law found in the Scripture, 'Love your neighbour as yourself,' you are doing right. But if you show favouritism, you sin and are convicted by the law as law-breakers.

This passage is often too true for comfort. The rich visitor is given priority over the poor, shabbily dressed visitor to church. James explains that God hates this. It is often the rich who exploit the poor and make them poorer. Treating someone differently because they are rich or poor, or by their looks, is just as much a sin as anything else.

Activities

1   Briefly outline and explain one Bible passage that a Christian could use to support the view that prejudice and discrimination are wrong. **C 2.2**

2   Why does James make favouritism such a wrong thing to do? What in fact could this lead to? Give reasons. **C 2.2, PS 2.1**

Exam questions to practise

Below are some sample exam questions for paper 2B. To help you score full marks, the first two questions are followed by some tips from examiners. Before attempting the remaining three questions, try to work out your own strategy for approaching them.

1   Explain how prejudice leads to discrimination. (3)

2   Why do Christians believe that prejudice is wrong? (3)

Now try questions 3, 4 and 5 on your own. Before you write your answers, spend some time thinking about your approach.

3   What can we learn from Jesus about our attitudes towards:
    a   people of a different race
    b   people who are disabled? (4)

4   'Getting rid of prejudice will create world peace.' Do you agree? Give reasons for your answer, showing you have thought about more than one point of view. Refer to Christianity. (5)

5   What did Jesus teach in the parable of the good Samaritan about prejudice and discrimination? (3)

How to score full marks

1   First you need to define prejudice and discrimination. Then you need to explain how prejudice leads to discrimination, making sure you give some examples.

2   This needs a Bible passage to support your answer.

War and peace

This section includes:

- War: an introduction
- Just war
- Effects and cost of war
- Christians and war
- Pacifism and non-violent protests
- Peace and war crimes
- Nuclear warfare
- Bible passages 1
- Bible passages 2
- Exam questions to practise

Statistics show that there has been no time of total world peace since 1945. If every country gave one day's arms spending to agencies such as Christian Aid, world famine and poverty could be almost solved overnight.

In this section, different attitudes to war will be considered, including pacifism. Protest and ways of getting across a point of view will also be discussed, with Bible references (mainly of the teaching of Jesus), which are not often easy to put into practice!

War: an introduction

Key terms

Civil war People of the same country form opposing sides and fight each other. The reasons for this could be religious or related to different ethnic groups that make up the same country.

Holy War Fought with the belief that God is on their side and wants them to fight.

War Armed conflict between two or more opposing groups.

Since 1945 there has not been one minute of total world peace. The nature of **war** has dramatically changed. Opposing sides used to face each other. But now, cruise missiles can be programmed to hit a target hundreds of miles away. In the past the majority of casualties were soldiers. However, in the Gulf War (1990) and subsequent conflicts, civilians have been used as human shields. The bombing of cities in World War II began the rise in **civilian** casualties.

War has many causes, often deep-rooted. There are no long-term winners in war and the same problems often surface again later. For example, countries in the Balkans were fighting in the nineteenth century. Wars broke out over the same issues throughout the twentieth century, culminating in horrific atrocities in the 1990s.

There are no winners in war, as the situation in Kosovo proves.

What causes a war?

- *Greed* is often a factor. One country wants land that belongs to another. Each country will provide proof of its claim somewhere in the past, however flimsy that proof may seem.

- *Racial problems*. Different races within the same country do not get on together and war breaks out – for example, the Kosovans and Serbians. Their dispute may be linked to historical problems. At the end of World Wars I and II, many countries were carved up, united or even created. People found themselves living where they did not even speak the same language. **Civil war** breaks out as these people begin to seek their independence again, for example in the Balkans after the break up of Yugoslavia.

- *Religion*. Most religions preach peace, yet it is a major cause of conflict. People of some religions find it difficult to understand different religions, for example, Hindus and Muslims in India or Pakistan. Sometimes the fighting is between factions of the same faith such as Christians (Protestants and Roman Catholics) in Northern Ireland.

- *To stop a tyrant or dictator*. Countries unite as allies in a quest to stop atrocities or the harbouring of terrorists. For example, in World War II, the aim was to stop Hitler and in 2001 the USA began to attack Afghanistan because they harboured the terrorists responsible for the attacks on the World Trade Centre in New York. Some people regard this as revenge so the topic is hotly debated.

Holy War

This is the idea of fighting a war in God's name. The most famous example of **Holy War** was 'The Age of Crusades', which took place in the Middle Ages. Christians went to the **Holy Land** to reclaim it from the pagan Muslims. Terrible attrocities were committed on *both* sides in the name of God.

Today, Jews fight Arabs in Israel, claiming God is on their side. Muslims in Afghanistan claim Allah is on their side when attacking the USA. Hindus and Muslims clash in India and Pakistan, and so the list goes on.

Peace-keeping: new role for troops

A new role for troops gradually developed at the end of the twentieth century. This is peace-keeping on behalf of NATO (the North Atlantic Treaty Organization) or the **United Nations (UN)**.

These troops wear pale blue berets to identify them. The soldiers do not take sides, aiming to keep the peace between two or more warring factions. One commanding officer controls all the troops.

The UK is always willing to send troops – for example, to Somalia, Rwanda and the former Yugoslavian states. They will be armed, but will only fire in self-defence.

Some experts are worried that the UK's high profile roles in several areas will put a strain on resources. Some 8,500 troops went to Kosovo and 12,000 are still on standby. An initial timescale for these troops was three years in Kosovo, which was then revised to 20 years. Indeed, a Foreign Office advisor said: 'I have just come back from Bosnia and I can tell you that if the peace-keeping force left the whole area would erupt.' (January 2001)

The British army has about 103,000 men and women, many committed round the world. There are still 15,000 in Northern Ireland, 5,000 in Bosnia, and a secret figure in the Falkland Islands and in the Gulf. The latest role for UK troops is for 3,000 to go to Afghanistan to help the new government establish itself.

Many soldiers serving in Bosnia and Kosovo are still traumatized as more atrocities (committed by all factions) are found. One well-documented incident was when a basement was unlocked and found to be full of the charred bodies of up to twenty Muslim men, women and children.

The question is: it is noble and all very well trying to keep peace, but is it worth it? Is Britain right to take a high profile role?

The blue beret: a symbol of peace-keeping forces in troubled areas.

Activities

1 Using the Internet and reference books, make a list of the wars since 1945. (Archive newspapers are a superb source of information. They can be found on newspaper websites.) For each war, list the following details. (You could even predict the result in a table.)
   a The names of the sides involved.
   b The causes of the war.
   c The type of war – for example, civil.
   d Which side (if any) won.
   e What happened in the end. **IT 2.3**

2 Choose one conflict from your list. Using a desktop publishing package on your computer, compile a newspaper article outlining the causes and results (including cost to civilians) of this conflict. Include pictures if you wish. **IT 2.2**

Key points

- War is complicated and caused by many factors.
- It is probably rare to find one side totally blameless.
- Historical factors often play a part in war.

Just war

Key terms

Just war Belief that it is right to fight. A Christian concept to justify war.

Just war is a theory that attempts to justify wars and also tries to limit war. The first part of the theory was drawn up by St Thomas Aquinas, a Christian theologian and writer of some influence in the thirteenth-century Church. He was, of course, writing it with medieval-type wars in mind.

What wars used to be like

Most wars in the thirteenth century had the two opposing armies camping at opposite ends of a battlefield. Soldiers on both sides would form lines or ranks at each end, cavalry at the back, archers at the front and foot soldiers in between. A trumpet would sound and the archers let loose. Hand-to-hand fighting was the norm. The winning side was the one that had the most men left or a surviving king.

In later years, opposing sides still faced each other but they used cannons instead of arrows. Armour got heavier and weapons development was big business.

In World War I, opposing sides still faced each other – albeit in trenches and with yet more lethal weapons, following the invention of the tank and the gas bomb.

World War II was really the first major war where the opposing sides did not always face each other on the battlefield. New tactics included air fighting,

In medieval times, the side with the most troops still alive was the winner.

bombing of cities and other civilian targets and the use of submarines to attack the Merchant Navy and Naval Ships.

The five rules of Just war

St Augustine wrote two criteria for Just war, but Aquinas is credited for writing them clearly and adding the philosophy. He also contributed the third criteria, 'right intention'. Other Christian philosophers debated new criteria over the next 500 years and, eventually, five rules were agreed. (Sometimes the rules are subdivided so that there are six or seven, but most commonly they are written as five.)

Christians are divided as to whether all five rules have to be in place for a war to be called 'just' or whether just one or two will do. Below is the list.

1. The war must be started and controlled by the state and/or its ruler – such as a king. This is also called the 'legitimate ruling authority'. An example of this is if the UK were to go to war with another country, it must be the government that decides as it is the 'legitimate ruling authority'.

2. There must be a just cause (reason) with a chance of winning – for example, war in defence of aggression and attack. In World War II, the Allies decided the cause was just, and defended countries from German attack. Some Christians do not think that the Gulf War was just. They claim it was less to do with defence and more to do with oil rights.

3. War must be a last resort after all other options have been exhausted and have a good chance of success. In World War II, the Allies believed they had tried all means of negotiation and had been duped. In the Gulf War, some Christians believe that not enough mediation was tried first.

4. The war must be to promote good and overcome evil. Peace and justice must be restored quickly. In World War II, the Allies believed that Hitler himself was evil, aiming for a superior race. In the Gulf War, most of the Allies believed Saddam Hussein to be evil but realized that the Iraqi people were suffering, especially when used as human shields in military sites.

War is only just if all other means of peaceful negotiation have failed.

5 Proportionality – only enough force should be used as is absolutely necessary to achieve peace. Innocent civilians should not be attacked. In World War I this aim was on the whole upheld, but by World War II civilians were targeted and whole cities bombed. In the Gulf War, the use of laser-guided missiles and bombs should have resulted in only military units being bombed. But Hussein rounded up civilians and locked them in these bases, and warned the coalition forces what he was going to do.

Laser-guided missiles: the weapons of modern warfare.

Saddam Hussein: is this the face of evil?

Activities

1 Look at your list from Activity 1 on page 83. Which wars do you think were just? Give reasons. **PS 2.1**

2 Why do you think civilians are often targeted in war? List your reasons. **PS 2.1**

3 Act out the following role play, which is also an exercise in empathy. You will need a maximum of six people to be committee members.

Imagine you are on a committee to review the Just war rules for the twenty-first century. You need to discuss whether you would keep the rules as they are, add to them or even cut them.

After some practice, act out your role play to the rest of the class.

C 2.1b, WO 2.1, 2.3

Key points

- There are five main rules of Just war. The rules developed as war tactics changed.
- The aim of the five rules is to make the cause of war acceptable and morally right.
- Just war is a Christian concept.

Effects and cost of war

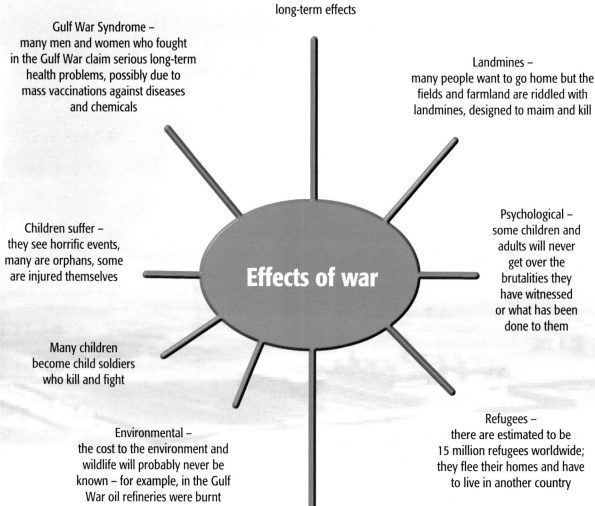

Ill-health –
some soldiers suffer for years
from the effects of gas bombs;
others suffer loss of limbs,
horrific burns and other
long-term effects

Gulf War Syndrome –
many men and women who fought
in the Gulf War claim serious long-term
health problems, possibly due to
mass vaccinations against diseases
and chemicals

Landmines –
many people want to go home but the
fields and farmland are riddled with
landmines, designed to maim and kill

Children suffer –
they see horrific events,
many are orphans, some
are injured themselves

Effects of war

Psychological –
some children and
adults will never
get over the
brutalities they
have witnessed
or what has been
done to them

Many children
become child soldiers
who kill and fight

Refugees –
there are estimated to be
15 million refugees worldwide;
they flee their homes and have
to live in another country

Environmental –
the cost to the environment and
wildlife will probably never be
known – for example, in the Gulf
War oil refineries were burnt

Shellshock –
in World War I many soldiers
were shot for cowardice or going
AWOL (absent without leave) when,
in fact, they were mentally ill; many
such soldiers have now been pardoned

The arms race: right or wrong?

In the UK, keeping the armed forces equipped and up to date does not come cheap. Millions of pounds are spent. In fact, in terms of expenditure, only the Health Service receives more. The British manufacture of weapons is a successful industry, employing more than one million people. Take a look at the following facts.

FACT £1.5 million is spent every minute globally on weapons.

FACT The West spends twenty per cent more on weapons than aid to developing countries.

FACT For every fifteen years that a person pays tax in UK, four of those years will have funded defence alone.

FACT War is the biggest cause of starvation, disability and poverty.

FACT A Tornado bomber costs £20 million minimum. This money could feed four million people for one month or almost completely fund the well-digging project in Africa enabling all the schemes to be completed.

FACT One guided missile costs almost £1 million. This money could send seeds, tools and experts to help 50 villages and solve their problems forever.

FACT Chemical weapons are banned but many developing countries have them instead of nuclear weapons. In 1988, Iraq gassed Halabja, killing 4,000 and seriously injuring 30,000. There is the fear this could happen again (which it did) – gas can be invisible and not smelt at all.

FACT The cost of one jet fighter would vaccinate more than three million children against all major diseases.

Many Christians support the updating of weaponry in the fear that if Britain is under-armed another country, perhaps seeking revenge, will attack. Others say that all events are controlled by God so he will protect those doing his will.

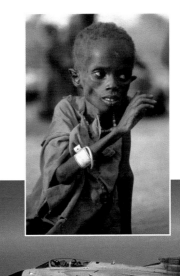

The real dilemma: is it best to fund war or a starving child?

Activities

1 Many civilian jobs are dependent on the armed forces. Make a list of the ones you can think of (for example, factories that make uniforms and boots). **PS 2.1**

2 Imagine that the government has decided to save money on defence. Your group (maximum, six people) is a committee that has been asked to draw up, in order of importance, how you would spend the money. You should have five to ten schemes, at home and/or abroad. Justify your choice. **C 2.1b, WO 2.1, 2.3**

3 Look at the effects of war on page 86. For each, write down how you could put it right. **PS 2.2**

Key points

• War is costly in many ways – in lost lives, in injuries, in psychological effects, in damage to the environment and in money.

• World poverty could probably be ended if armament spending was cut.

Christians and war

Some Christians believe there are justifiable reasons for fighting a war. Others do not. Some say the teachings of Jesus do not really offer any clear guidelines, because he never actually said that all wars are wrong.

Why Christians might fight

- They may believe the cause is justified. It might be in defence of a weaker country.

- They may follow what Paul says in Romans 13 about the ruling authorities. Paul says God has put the rulers where they are so Christians should obey them. This could be developed by saying if you are called up to serve, then you must obey. God is behind what is happening. He is in ultimate control.

- They may wish to defend their family. They do not want their family to be under foreign rule.

- They may wish to serve their country. They have national pride to defend. **Nationalism** is devotion to your country but in recent years it has been used more in the context of wanting independence for your country. **Jingoism** goes one step further and is aggressive nationalism, which leads to extreme stances – for example, there is often the desire to rid the nation of ethnic minorities or of anyone seen as 'different', and racism becomes rife.

- They may want to overthrow a tyrant or dictator seen as a threat to world peace or who is persecuting Christians.

- They may agree with their country defending another country from aggression. Christians wish to defend fellow Christians.

Why Christians might not fight

- They are **pacifists** who believe all wars and fighting are wrong.

- They are **conscientious objectors** who believe a particular war is wrong. They feel they cannot go against their conscience and fight. There will be many reasons, such as the belief that a particular war has nothing to do with their country, the cause is not just, their country is being greedy. Summed up, they do not believe the government is right to declare war.

- They have no desire to die fighting. They may be scared. Nor do they wish to kill. Christians believe in, and try to keep, the Ten Commandments. One says 'Do not kill'. Even if it was a case of 'kill or be killed', it does not make killing right.

- They believe it is a waste of resources – for example, what one country spends on weapons could solve world starvation almost overnight.

- They know war causes untold suffering to many – families, civilians and the environment (including the 'enemy' side).

Was Jesus a pacifist?

There was no such word as pacifism in the time of Jesus. However, scholars study the words and actions of Jesus to see if there is evidence of pacifist thinking and teaching. Needless to say in the end it is a personal choice and interpretation because Jesus never actually said 'All wars are wrong!'

The cost of war is great to both sides.

No, he wasn't

- In Mark 11: 15–18 (The traders in the temple) – see page 98 – Jesus drove out the traders in anger. There is no evidence to report that any person was hurt. But it is his actions that brought Jesus into conflict with the authorities. Many modern-day pacifists say that even knocking over tables and driving the merchants out is not true pacifism.

- Nowhere in the gospel does Jesus say that all war is wrong and that you should not fight.

- Jesus often changed or added to Old Testament teaching. In the Old Testament there is mention of hundreds of wars where the Israelites believed God was on their side, giving them sometimes miraculous victories and, as was the norm at the time, often completely wiping out the losing city or tribe – men, women and children. Jesus did not single out wars to change its teaching. He told people to love their enemies. Many scholars would argue that 'enemies' refers here to your personal enemy rather than the nation's enemy.

- Jesus had at least one Zealot as a disciple – Simon the Zealot. They wanted an outright war against the Romans, to totally annihilate them.

- In Luke 4: 16–21 (The spirit of the Lord) – see page 96 – Jesus said the spirit of the Lord was on him, proclaiming freedom of prisoners, releasing the oppressed. Many say that this can hardly be peaceful.

Yes, he was

- In his teaching in Matthew 5: 38–42, he tells people to 'turn the other cheek' – the principle of not retaliating.

- In the Beatitudes in Matthew 5: 9, he says, 'Blessed are the peacemakers; for they will be called sons of God.' They are important people, they are 'sons'.

- In Matthew 26: 47–53 (The arrest of Jesus) – see page 97 – when Jesus was arrested and Peter attacked on his behalf, Jesus said that violence will only breed violence. His words were: 'All who take the sword will die by the sword.' Jesus reminded Peter that if God so wished he had a legion of angels to defend him.

- When Jesus entered Jerusalem he rode in on a donkey. He was not coming as a warrior king on a horse, he was coming as a king of peace on a common donkey.

- In Matthew 5: 43–8, Jesus speaks about the treatment of enemies and reverses the norm, saying, 'Care for your enemies and pray for those who persecute you'.

Activities

1 What would be your main reason for:
   a fighting in a war
   b not fighting in a war?
   Give reasons for your responses.
   C 2.1a, PS 1.2

2 Note down why you think many teenagers want to join the armed forces. What is the appeal? You could find some recruitment posters and try to work out the tactics behind the pictures and slogans. There are also several websites that you could visit.
   C 2.3, IT 2.1

3 Do you think Jesus was a pacifist or not? Give your own reasons and list other evidence. **PS 2.1**

Key points

- Many Christians would have to think long and hard to decide if they would fight in a war or not.

- Retaliation is a basic human reaction, so Jesus makes it clear what we should do.

- Christians who decide to fight might quote from Romans 13, which tells them to obey their governments.

- Christians who decide not to fight might be pacifists or they might not think the cause is just.

- It remains undecided whether Jesus was a pacifist or not.

Pacifism and non-violent protests

The idea of pacifism has developed over the centuries. Jesus taught about peace and he refused to retaliate at his arrest. Medieval Christian philosophers and writers began to try to reconcile Jesus' and the Early Christians' rejection of war with the need to fight for political power. This led St Aquinas to the doctrine of Just war.

Who are pacifists?

The Society of Friends (Quakers) are pacifists. They believe that there is something of God in all people and that to achieve results you appeal to this inner ability to love and to do good. In 1661 their Peace Testimony was written. It said:

> The Spirit of Christ, which leads us into all truth, will never move us to fight war against any man with outward weapons.

In World War I, pacifists were treated as traitors. Those who refused to fight were often forcibly sent to the front line or shot. Others were put in prison camps. The media stirred up the situation – women began sending white feathers (which represented cowardice) in the post to known pacifists. Sometimes men who could not fight for other reasons, such as a medical disability or illness, or having a reserved occupation (such as farmers) were also subjected to hatred.

In fact, pacifists were not cowards. Many served in areas of great danger – for example, as stretcher bearers on the front line and as ambulance drivers.

White feathers are the symbol for cowardice, yet pacifists were often brave for holding on to their beliefs.

Dietrich Bonhoeffer (1906–1945)
Bonhoeffer lived in Germany. He trained to be a **Lutheran** pastor and theologian. When he began to preach, Nazi Germany was gaining strength. Bonhoeffer preached the message of pacifism and joined in non-violent protests against Hitler.

He found out about the treatment of Jews in Germany and began to help them escape to countries like Switzerland. He used his contacts to spread information about the **Resistance** movement throughout Europe. Bonhoeffer provided false papers. He began to realize that Hitler was not going to listen to peaceful protests.

He began to revise his Christian beliefs about pacifism. He joined a group working to end Nazism and took part in the plot to assassinate Hitler in 1944. He was arrested and taken to the Gestapo prison in Berlin. After that he was moved to Buchenwald Camp, then on to Flossenburg Concentration Camp. He and other 'traitors' were hanged on 9 April 1945.

The SS doctor who witnessed Bonhoeffer's death said, 'He was devout, brave and composed … his death ensued after a few seconds, submissive to God's will.'

Bonhoeffer's final message to a friend in England said: 'This is the end for my body, but for me the beginning of life.'

Bonhoeffer was a Christian pacifist who developed a belief that violence is evil, but there are worse evils and the only way to deal with them is by using violence. Unfortunately his work was unfinished and his ideas were incomplete. But he did write about the 'greater evil' and that it could not be defeated by pacifism.

Non-violent protest

This is closely linked to pacifism as an alternative to violence. The great Indian leader Mahatma Gandhi worked on the idea in his opposition to British rule in India (although he cannot be used as a Christian example). Martin Luther King read books about non-violent protest in detail and developed his ideas in his fight against racism in the USA.

One common error is the belief that no one gets killed or hurt during non-violent protests. Indeed, the protesters may set out with the aim of peace, but their opposition (such as the riot police or the army) usually have the opposite view. People – often those protesting peacefully – do get hurt and are sometimes killed.

Examples of non-violent protest

Some non-violent actions are heroic, for example, in Tiananmen Square in 1989. Chinese students held a candlelit vigil as part of a series of peaceful protests against repression in China and to support freedom and democracy within China and other communist countries such as Russia. The Chinese leaders, Deng Xiaoping, Li Peng and others ordered army tanks to clear the Square. The protesters stood where they were. Some tanks steered clear, but one advanced. A young man refused to move, the tank moved on, the student was mown down.

Many non-violent actions are dramatic – for example, people entering nuclear testing sites, people on ice-floats spraying harmless dye on seal pups to prevent their slaughter for their skins, and people entering air bases and sitting on the runways.

Some non-violent actions will involve thousands of people and the aim is to instil a sense of their own power for change – for example, mass demonstrations such as boycotts and strikes.

This brave civilian was mown down and killed by an Army tank in Tiananmen Square.

Some non-violent actions take place in the quiet – for example, shipbuilders in Nazi-occupied Denmark decided to 'misunderstand' orders (language problems!) and did their work so badly that the ships they were building were useless for war. There were many similar stories, such as radio builders making mistakes, which meant the radios could only transmit or receive, and bomb factory workers building errors into the weapons, such as making them self-destruct.

What Christians believe

Christians accept that non-violent protest may achieve results slowly, but gradually protest will wear away at the oppressor. Vaclav Havel was a Czech playwright, imprisoned for his political beliefs. However, due to popular non-violent action, such as candlelit vigils, he was released, the government collapsed and he became the new president.

Other Christians accept that violent action may be the lesser evil and that it may be justified.

Activities

1   Do you think Bonhoeffer was right in his developing views? Give reasons. **PS 2.1**

2   Act out the following role play. You will need two people – a pacifist and his girlfriend.

   The couple are discussing/arguing why the pacifist will not fight in World War II. The girlfriend is planning to send him a white feather with a picture of the two of them. How do the conversations develop? Practise the role play, then act it out for the rest of the class. **WO 2.2, 2.3**

Key points

- Some non-violent protests make the headlines. Other tactics go on behind the scenes.
- It is untrue to say nobody gets hurt or killed. The protesters will aim for peace, but their opponents usually have the opposite attitude.

Peace and war crimes

Peaceful conflict resolution

Respect the right to disagree;
Express your real concerns;
Share common goals and interests;
Open yourself to different points of view;
Listen carefully to all proposals;
Understand the major issues involved;
Think about probable consequences;
Imagine several possible alternative
  solutions;
Offer some reasonable compromises;
Negotiate mutually fair cooperative
  agreements.

(The Festival Shop)

Peace

Many Christians believe that following Jesus gives them peace with God and thus peace within themselves. Jesus taught that peace is a sign of the **kingdom of God**. It means getting rid of injustice, hunger and ill-treatment of humans and the environment. It means Christians want to help others rather than get revenge, trying to understand the points of view of others.

Jesus taught you should forgive, not threaten. Peace is God's gift. For example, in John 14: 27, Jesus said: 'Peace I leave with you…'

The key to peace is forgiveness. If people do not forgive, there is no peace. Jesus taught many parables about God forgiving us regardless of what we have done. Jesus said that if we are angry with someone then we should not approach the altar until it is settled. On a national theme, God's kingdom is peace and countries at war do not show his kingdom.

Inner peace and silent prayers

During **Holy Communion** Christians ask for inner peace: 'Christ is our peace. He has reconciled us to God in one body by the cross. We meet in his name and share his peace.'

The congregation then share the peace with each other. Many Christians believe that if you are in dispute with someone when you come to Holy Communion, then you should not receive it while there is not peace in your heart. Some churches have a Peace chapel or quiet area, with lighted candles, lists of conflicts and pictures of hostages worldwide. This encourages prayers for peace at home and abroad.

In the quiet of a Peace chapel, it is often easier to think about inner peace or say silent prayers.

War crimes

There are some people who believe that in war there are no rules. Anything is acceptable as long as you win. But if there are no rules, why are there war crimes and wanted war criminals? If there are no rules then you cannot break them, so no crimes are committed. Many would totally disagree and point out there are rules, such as the Just war conditions and the 1949 Geneva Conventions (see below) which includes rules on the treatment of captured soldiers.

During World War I, it was accepted that some violations of the rules of war were crimes. In 1945, the Charter of the International Military Tribunal at Nuremberg gave a definition of war crimes as: 'Violations of rules or customs of war, including murder and deportation of civilians and the killing of hostages.'

In 1949, the Geneva Conventions included a set of defined war crimes. The list of war crimes includes the following:

- Deliberate killing, torture and inhumane treatment, such as doing experiments on prisoners.
- Deliberately causing suffering to mind and body.
- Depriving prisoners of war of the rights of a fair and public trial (also includes civilian prisoners).

- Unlawful deportation of civilians (called ethnic cleansing today).
- The taking of hostages.

In 1977, some new categories were added, including:

- Making civilians objects of attack by forcing them to go to military bases or weapon factories (called human shields).
- Delaying sending back prisoners of war.
- Not giving all prisoners a fair trial with translators.

From the beginning, lawyers tried to get round a definition or a rule. 'Many crimes considered "grave" are not defined as such.' It was also argued that this did not apply to civil war. In the 1990s, additional violations were written down – including rape, mutilation, starvation in camps, beatings, indecent assault and being forced to perform homosexual acts.

The Nuremberg Trials convicted many Nazi war criminals. Their defence was that they had to obey orders. This was not accepted. The judges said that each individual is responsible for his or her own actions.

Bosnia War Crimes Tribunal

In the first international war crimes trial since World War II, Bosnian Serb Dusko Tadic was charged with crimes related to the rape, torture and murder of prisoners in and around three prison camps in North Bosnia. After 78 days of court, the trial of Tadic ended on 28 November 1996.

A panel of three judges reached a unanimous verdict on 7 May 1997, finding Tadic guilty on eleven counts of persecution and beatings. On 14 July 1997, he was sentenced to twenty years in prison, with the recommendation to serve at least ten years.

Dusko Tadic: a modern-day war criminal.

Other war criminals

Many war criminals are still at large. Three notable examples are given below:

- Radovan Karadzic – President of Serbian Democratic party. He and Ratko Mladic are charged with the internment of thousands of non-Serbians in concentration camps and subjecting them to inhumane treatment, ordering sniper fire on civilians and using them as human shields, and the seizure of 284 UN peacekeepers with the aim of using them as shields in June 1996. In April 2001 he was arrested on war crimes charges and his trial is proceeding.
- Ratko Mladic – General of Serbian armed forces. Charged as Karadzic and further charged with genocide (ordering the massacre of 6,000 Muslims in Srebrenica in July 1995).
- Slobodan Milosevic – President of Serbia. Charged with crimes against humanity and violation of the rules of war.

Activities

1 Try to explain what you think 'inner peace' means. **C 1.1a**

2 Do you think war criminals should receive the death penalty? Give reasons. **C 2.1a**

3 In your own words explain in detail the term 'war crime'. **PS 2.1, 2.2**

4 Do you agree with the soldiers' defence that they had to obey orders or the judges that you are responsible for your own actions? Give reasons. **PS 2.1**

Key points

- Jesus taught about peace, including inner peace. He said that peace is a sign of the kingdom of God, and that the key to peace is forgiveness.
- Some people argue that there are no rules in war – you do what you can to win. Others argue that there are, and that by breaking these rules you become a criminal.

Nuclear warfare

The atomic bomb

People are still suffering the effects today of a bomb dropped in 1945.

In August 1945, the USA dropped atomic (nuclear) bombs on the Japanese cities of Hiroshima and Nagasaki. Hundreds of thousands of civilians died. Many more suffered the effects of radiation. Even today deformed babies are born to women who were not born in 1945. These deformities are directly attributable to those bombs and there are still large areas where cancer is commonplace.

Supporters of the USA said the atomic bomb ended the war, stopped the slaughter and horrific (and well-documented) treatment of prisoners of war by the Japanese and avoided further casualties.

Other nuclear weapons

Since the atomic bomb, countries have developed bigger, more destructive and more accurate **nuclear weapons**. There is still an unspoken fear they could be used.

With the ending of the Cold War in the 1980s, many countries signed a treaty banning the testing of nuclear weapons as the threat of nuclear war subsided. In the late 1990s, some Asian states and Pakistan tested nuclear weapons confirming they now have the technology.

During the Cold War people began to debate whether it was morally right to have nuclear weapons as a deterrent. If two countries had them, the idea was that neither side would use them or fire first. Concern was raised about their acquisition by more 'unstable regimes'. Many Christians and non-Christians alike began to call for **disarmament**.

Nuclear disarmament

- Nuclear disarmament refers to the giving up of nuclear weapons.
- Multilateral nuclear disarmament is when all countries get rid of their nuclear weapons together by agreement.
- Staged multilateral nuclear disarmament is when, for example, two countries agree that one will give up twenty nuclear warheads at the same time as the other gives up twenty, and independent weapons inspectors will be in both countries to oversee the process.
- Unilateral nuclear disarmament is when one country takes a lead and disarms, regardless of what others do, in the hope of shaming other countries to do so too. This was seen as very risky and foolish by many groups, including Christians, as it could leave your country open to attack and defenceless against nuclear might. Terrorist groups could hold the country to ransom.

The Church and the bomb

The Church of England debated the whole issue of nuclear weapons in 1982. The document published said the Church should give a moral lead to the UK rather than decide the actual defence policy.

- It was the government's duty to keep enough forces to prevent nuclear blackmail.
- Policy and tactics should be defensive in nature.
- It could never be morally right to even use a small nuclear bomb.
- All countries, especially those in **NATO**, should agree to sign an agreement specifying they would never be the first to use a nuclear weapon.
- Nuclear stockpiles should be destroyed.

Campaign for Nuclear Disarmament (CND)

Bruce Kent

CND was founded in 1958, and first used its distinguishing logo a few months later. CND supported unilateral nuclear disarmament as it believed multilateral ways were not working. It highlighted the dangers of the USA, the former Soviet Union, the UK, France and China stockpiling weapons. It particularly highlighted the danger of accidents.

In the 1980s, CND became popular again. It was led by Monsignor Bruce Kent, a Roman Catholic priest. He gave up the priesthood to devote himself to CND as General Secretary. He developed the idea that to use, or threaten to use, nuclear weapons went against Christian teaching regarding the sanctity of life. He also ensured that supporters used non-violent protest tactics.

CND put forward various views against nuclear weapons such as the following:

- Countries like Japan have spent their resources on building up industry rather than on defence and they have become very wealthy.

- The money spent on weapons could be spent on feeding the starving people of the world.

- The risk of nuclear accidents continues to rise. The consequences were seen at the Chernobyl nuclear power station accident in 1986.

New weapons of fear and death

Defence Secretary of the USA, William Cohen, said in 2000:

> A lone madman or group of terrorists with a bottle of chemicals, or a batch of plague inducing bacteria, can threaten to kill tens of thousands.

William Cohen was talking about a new fear, that of attacks with chemical and biological weapons. The USA reports monthly that they have found evidence of increasing stores of chemical and biological weapons and countries doing further research, usually under the guise of medicine factories.

Many weapons advisers call these **weapons of mass destruction** the 'poor man's nukes'. Chemical and biological weapons are relatively cheap to produce, yet they are powerful enough to destroy thousands, even millions, of people. Once released, many of these chemicals will be undetectable. Effects on humans range from choking, vomiting, extreme stomach pains, numbing of the body, and contracting and cramping of muscles.

During the Gulf War in the early 1990s, Saddam Hussein's troops gassed Kurdish civilian refugees in Iraq, using a chemical nerve agent. People in Iran died, too, as the wind blew the gas across the border.

All Christian denominations have condemned even the thought of using these weapons. Some Christians went so far as to call on the UN to order air strikes on illegal stockpiles and research establishments.

Activities

1 Take a look at the information CND website (www.cnduk.org). Do you think CND has been successful or not? Give reasons. **IT 2.1**

2 Do you think it was right for Bruce Kent to give up the priesthood to lead a non-Christian organization? Give reasons. **C 2.1a**

Key points

- The nuclear threat has receded between countries like the USA and Russia, but there is a new fear of less stable countries using nuclear weapons.

- The latest threat is chemical and biological weapons used by states who do not care that they are illegal.

Here you will find the relevant Bible passages that you will need for the war and peace section. The set passages are written out, then there is an explanation of what they mean.

Matthew 5: 38–48 (Teaching on forgiveness)

This passage is written out in full on page 56.

It is very easy to retaliate and seek revenge when it is an individual who goes against another. It is just as much an issue when it is one country against another. Jesus is teaching Christians to be different and not do what everyone else does.

Jesus tells us to avoid situations that could lead to conflict. He says that God treats everyone equally and fairly, regardless of whether some people think of others as more sinful or not. We too must aim to be like Jesus and do the same.

Jesus sets us a difficult task. It is harder to walk away from violence, perhaps harder still to keep away from conflict and even more so to love your enemies.

Romans 13: 1–7 (The authority of the state)

Everyone must submit himself to the governing authorities, for there is no authority except that which God has established. The authorities that exist have been established by God. Consequently, he who rebels against the authority is rebelling against what God has instituted, and those who do so will bring judgement on themselves. For rulers hold no terror for those who do right, but for those who do wrong. Do you want to be free from fear of the one in authority? Then do what is right and he will commend you. For he is God's servant to do you good. But if you do wrong, be afraid, for he does not bear the sword for nothing. He is God's servant, an agent of wrath to bring punishment on the wrongdoer.

Therefore, it is necessary to submit to the authorities, not only because of possible punishment but also because of conscience. This is also why you pay taxes, for the authorities are God's servants, who give their full time to governing. Give everyone what you owe him: If you owe taxes, pay taxes; if revenue, then revenue; if respect, then respect; if honour, then honour.

Christians must obey their government (ruling authority) by keeping laws and paying taxes. They must be 'law abiding' citizens. God is in control and He put the ruler there. Today we might call the ruler a king, a prime minister or a president.

Paul says if we disobey the ruler, we disobey God. If you break the law, then you deserve punishment. However, no ruler is entitled to make a person go against his or her conscience.

The problem with this passage is what if the ruler goes against Christianity? For example, in communist Russia Christianity was banned, church services (except in some **Orthodox Churches**) were banned, using Bibles was banned … and so the list went on. Many Christians broke the law of their land by just being Christian. They worshipped together in houses and some people smuggled in Bibles for them. The question was should they break the law? And should they put others at risk by their actions?

There were some who believed the Bible smugglers were fool-hardy and were putting the lives of ordinary people at risk. Others actively helped the smugglers and believed they were right to do so as the government was making people go against their consciences.

Luke 4: 16–21 (The spirit of the Lord)

[Jesus] went to Nazareth, where he had been brought up, and on the Sabbath day he went in to the synagogue, as was his custom. He stood up to read. The scroll of the prophet Isaiah was handed to him. Unrolling it, he found the place where it is written:

'The Spirit of the Lord is on me, because he has anointed me to preach good news to the poor. He has sent me to proclaim freedom for the prisoners and recovery of sight for the blind, to release the oppressed, to proclaim the year of the Lord's favour.'

Then he rolled up the scroll, gave it back to the attendant and sat down. The eyes of everyone in the synagogue were fastened on him, and he began by saying to them, 'Today this scripture is fulfilled in your hearing.'

Jesus is explaining a passage from his scriptures, the Jewish **Tenakh**. Christians call it the Old Testament. It was normal practice in a synagogue for a passage to be read and a teacher (rabbi), scholar or important person asked to talk about it.

Jesus is clear about his mission. He is there to help the poor, and the people that nobody wants to care about. He will free prisoners and the oppressed. Many Christians take this to mean those imprisoned wrongly or because they are in debt or who have been sent to prison without a fair trial.

Reading this, some Christians say that it is hardly showing pacifist tendencies. If you are going to free people you will end up fighting. But others say that the passage makes no reference to tactics, and non-violent methods could be used. What is clear is Christ's mission to the poor and down-trodden.

These words are often used by supporters of Liberation theology in South America, where the church is actively involved in fighting for the poor people, getting involved in politics and using violence if needed.

Matthew 26: 47–53 (The arrest of Jesus)

While [Jesus] was still speaking, Judas, one of the Twelve arrived. With him was a large crowd armed with swords and clubs, sent from the chief priests and the elders of the people. Now the betrayer had arranged a signal with them: 'The one I kiss is the man; arrest him!' Going at once to Jesus, Judas said, 'Greetings, Rabbi!' and kissed him.

Jesus replied, 'Friend, do what you came for.' Then the men stepped forward, seized Jesus and arrested him. With that, one of Jesus'

companions reached for his sword, drew it out and struck the servant of the high priest, cutting off his ear.

'Put your sword back in its place,' Jesus said to him, 'for all who draw the sword will die by the sword. Do you think I cannot call on my Father, and he will at once put at my disposal more than twelve legions of angels? But how then would the Scriptures be fulfilled that say it must happen in this way?'

At that time Jesus said to the crowd, 'Am I leading a rebellion, that you have to come out with swords and clubs to capture me? Every day I sat in the temple courts teaching, and you did not arrest me. But this has all taken place that the writing of the prophets might be fulfilled.' Then all the disciples deserted him and fled.

This passage can also be used in the section on love and forgiveness. We are told by John that it was Peter who wielded the sword in an effort to protect Jesus, who stopped him fearing that his action would most certainly result in his death. People who support pacifism use this to show Jesus as a man of peace, as he knew that violence would lead to death.

The key point in this is 'All who take the sword will die by the sword'. In today's language, this could be interpreted as this: 'Those who live by the gun will die by the gun', or something similar. Summed up, it means that violence breeds violence. Jesus then pointed out that if he had wanted God could have sent a huge army of angels.

Activities

1 In groups, work out five examples of occasions when Christians might decide it is right to break the law of the land. One is given in the explanation of Romans 13. (Breaking the speed limit to get to hospital is not the sort of example needed here.) **WO 2.1, 2.3**

2 Using a concordance or similar publication, make a list of occasions when Jesus broke the religious and/or state laws. **IT 2.1, PS 2.1**

3 In your own words try to explain what Jesus was saying in Luke 4: 16–21 (The spirit of the Lord). **C 2.2**

Passages (cont.)

Mark 11: 15–18 (The traders in the temple)

On reaching Jerusalem, Jesus entered the temple area and began driving out those who were buying and selling there. He overturned the tables of the money changers and the benches of those selling doves, and would not allow anyone to carry merchandise through the temple courts. And as he taught them, he said, 'Is it not written: "My house will be called a house of prayer for all nations"? But you have made it into a den of robbers.'

The chief priests and the teachers of the law heard this and began looking for a way to kill him, for they feared him, because the whole crowd was amazed at his teaching.

Jesus was angry that traders and priests were cheating the most vulnerable people who wanted to make sacrifices in the temple. The very people who should be helping the poor were encouraging the cheating. Jesus took action and drove them out.

People who believe Jesus was a pacifist and those who think he was not both use this passage to support their ideas.

Those who think he showed pacifist tendencies say that no one got hurt. He just overturned their tables and drove them out. He made his point. But those who say Jesus was not a pacifist say this is showing anger and the traders ran out before he hit them with a whip (another gospel says he picked up a whip). If they had stayed they would have been beaten. So they would say he displayed emotion, as he could not just stand by and see God's house being misused. It is called 'justified anger'.

Micah 4: 1–3

In the last days the mountain of the Lord's temple will be established as chief among the mountains; it will be raised above the hills, and peoples will stream to it.

Many nations will come and say, 'Come, let us go up to the mountain of the Lord, to the house of the God of Jacob. He will teach us his ways, so that we may walk in his paths.' The law will go out from Zion, the word of the Lord from Jerusalem. He will judge between many peoples and will settle disputes for strong nations far and wide. They will beat their swords into ploughshares and their spears into pruning hooks. Nation will not take up sword against nation, nor will they train for war any more.

Micah 5: 2–4

But you, Bethlehem Ephrathah, though you are small among the clans of Judah, out of you will come for me one who will be ruler over Israel, whose origins are from of old, from ancient times. Therefore Israel will be abandoned until the time when she who is in labour gives birth and the rest of his brothers return to join the Israelites. He will stand and shepherd his flock in the strength of the Lord, in the majesty of the name of the Lord his God. And they will live securely, for then his greatness will reach to the ends of the earth. He will be their peace.

Micah looks into the future, to a time of peace symbolized by swords and implements of war becoming farming tools. Disputes between nations will be resolved. Micah predicts the coming of the Messiah (the ruler over Israel) and describes him as a shepherd. Jesus often referred to himself as a shepherd, especially in John's gospel. Shepherds could be regarded as the opposite of soldiers.

Isaiah 58: 6–10

Is not this the kind of fasting I have chosen: to loose the chains of injustice and untie the cords of the yoke, to set the oppressed free and break every yoke? Is it not to share your food with the hungry and to provide the poor wanderer with shelter – when you see the naked, to clothe him, and not to turn away from your own flesh and blood? Then your light will break forth like the dawn, and your healing will quickly appear; then your righteousness will go before you, and the glory of the Lord will be your rear guard. Then you will call, and the Lord will answer; you will cry for help, and he will say: Here am I. If you do away with the yoke of oppression, with the pointing finger and malicious talk, and if you spend yourselves on behalf of the hungry and satisfy the needs of the oppressed, then your light will rise in the darkness, and your night will become like the noonday.

God is concerned about the poor, the hungry and those who received injustice. When peace comes the needs of everyone will be met. Isaiah talks about light in the darkness. Again, Jesus often said he was a light in the darkness. In Luke 4, Jesus reads out this passage from Isaiah 58, saying that it refers to him.

Romans 12: 9–21

Love must be sincere. Hate what is evil; cling to what is good. Be devoted to one another in brotherly love…. Share with God's people who are in need. Practise hospitality.

Bless those who persecute you; bless and do not curse. Rejoice with those who rejoice; mourn with those who mourn. Live in harmony with one another. Do not be proud, but be willing to associate with people of low position. Do not be conceited.

Do not repay anyone evil for evil. Be careful to do what is right in the eyes of everybody. If it is possible, as far as it depends on you, live in peace with everyone. Do not take revenge, my friends, but leave room for God's wrath, for it is written: 'It is mine to avenge; I will repay,' says the Lord. On the contrary: 'If your enemy is hungry, feed him; if he is thirsty, give him something to drink. In doing this you will heap burning coals on his head.' Do not be overcome by evil, but overcome evil with good.

Paul wants us to live in peace with everyone. He recommends we leave revenge to God, who will do the judging. Instead we must look after our enemies – feed them, give them a drink, generally care for them. Paul says we must overcome evil with good.

James 2: 1–9

My brothers, as believers in our glorious Lord Jesus Christ, don't show favouritism. Suppose a man comes into your meeting wearing a gold ring and fine clothes, and a poor man in shabby clothes also comes in. If you show special attention to the man wearing fine clothes and say, 'Here's a good seat for you,' but say to the poor man, 'You stand there' or 'Sit on the floor by my feet,' have you not discriminated among yourselves and become judges with evil thoughts? Listen, my dear brothers: Has not God chosen those who are poor in the eyes of the world to be rich in faith and to inherit the kingdom he promised those who love him? But you have insulted the poor. Is it not the rich who are exploiting you? Are they not the ones who are dragging you into court? Are they not the ones who are slandering the noble name of him to whom you belong?

If you really keep the royal law found in Scripture, 'Love you neighbour as yourself,' you are doing right. But if you show favouritism, you sin and are convicted by the law as law-breakers.

James warns Christians not to show favouritism in a meeting by treating a rich person as someone special and a poor person as a nobody, telling him he can sit on the floor. He says that the rich often exploit the poor. James clearly sees a link with disputes that start from lack of respect – that can lead to war.

Matthew 5: 9

Blessed are the peacemakers, for they will be called sons of God.

Jesus commends those who try to make peace. They are privileged and are called sons of God.

Activities

1   Make a list of some contemporary examples of 'justified anger'. **C 2.1a**

2   Re-read the passages in this section, then in your own words describe what world peace would be like. **C 2.2, PS 1.2**

Exam questions to practise

Below are some sample exam questions for paper 2B. To help you score full marks, the first three questions are followed by some tips from examiners. Before attempting the remaining two questions, try to work out your own strategy for approaching them.

1 Explain why some Christians believe that Jesus was a pacifist. (7)
(AQA 2000, C7a)

2 Explain why some Christians might think it right to fight in a war. (4)

3 Explain the conditions that need to be met for a Just war. You should include some examples. (8)

Now try questions 4 and 5 on your own. Before you write your answers, spend some time thinking about your approach.

4 Explain why some Christians believe that fighting a war is always wrong. (4)

5 **a** Explain how Christians could settle disputes between two countries without the use of violence. (6)

b Explain two drawbacks of non-violent protest. (4)

c What did Jesus teach about our attitude towards enemies? (4)

d 'It takes more courage to be a pacifist than to fight in a war.' Do you agree? Give reasons for your answer showing you have thought about more than one point of view. (5)

How to score full marks

1 Notice that this is worth seven marks, so there is plenty of chance to write enough to explain each point. You will need lots of Bible back up here.

2 Think of reasons why people fight in a war, but do not number them (1, 2, 3), as it will just look like a list.

3 Do not set out as a numbered list or bullet points. If you do not give examples you will be penalized.

Personal issues relating to the sacraments 1

This section includes:

- Baptism
- Confirmation
- The Eucharist
- Bible passages
- Exam questions to practise.

In this section the three sacraments of baptism, confirmation and the Eucharist will be discussed. The focus is on personal response. If I, as a parent, have my child baptized, how does it affect the way I act and the way I bring up my child? How does it affect my life if I make my own commitment to Christ through confirmation? If I take communion, say the Peace and repent of my sins, what affect should it have on my daily life?

The Sacrament of Reconciliation was dealt with in the chapter about forgiveness, where it was felt it had more context and relevance.

Baptism

Baptism is accepted as a sacrament instituted (begun and commanded) by Jesus himself by all denominations, except the Quakers. There are two main differences between denominations: *When?* Baby or older person? *How?* Sprinkled or total **immersion**?

Jesus is baptized

John the Baptist baptized Jesus, at his request, although he was sinless. One account is in Matthew 3: 13–17. It was his act of commitment to serve God. In the early church, baptism was for those who believed and wished to declare their faith. Some references are: Matthew 28: 19; Acts 2: 37, 38, 41; Acts 8: 34–9 and Romans 6: 7.

Why are babies baptized?

One idea about the origins of infant baptism is that Emperor Constantine decreed his empire Christian and all his subjects were to be baptized. Today Baptists and Pentecostalists are the main denominations that only baptize believers.

Baptism in a Roman Catholic Church

- The priest, parents and **godparents** make the sign of the cross on the child's forehead, a sign that the child belongs to Christ and has been saved by his death.
- The priest exorcizes (gets rid of evil spirits) and anoints the child, a sign that in the future the child will reject evil.

- The parents and godparents make promises and declare their faith on behalf of the child.

  I turn to Christ, I repent of my sins, I reject Satan, I believe in God the Father, the Almighty and Creator;
  I believe in Jesus, his son, who was crucified but rose from the dead;
  I believe in the Holy Spirit;
  I believe in the Catholic church, in the forgiveness of sins, in the resurrection of the body and in the life everlasting.

- The priest pours water from the font on the child's head three times, while saying, '*I baptize you in the name of the Father, the Son and the Holy Spirit*'. Water is a sign of cleansing.

- The priest anoints the child with chrism, a sign that the child is now a member of the body of Christ, the Church, to share its life.

- The priest lights a candle from the Paschal candle, which is given to the parents on behalf of their child saying, '*Receive the light of Christ*'. The candle is a sign that Christ will now guide the child to lead a Christian life and to be a light to the world.

The role of parents and godparents

Parents and godparents make promises on behalf of the baby who cannot understand what is happening. Their role does not end after the baptism, but is ongoing. There are several things they could do:

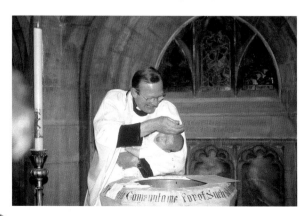

- Parents and godparents have to teach the child about Christian beliefs and values. One way is to read a Bible story at bedtime.

- Sometimes godparents take the child to church if the parents have to work. If they attend another church, it gives the child the chance to see a different way of doing things.

- The hope is that one day the child will go forward for confirmation.

- Godparents do not promise to care for the child should the parents die.

The candle

Receive this light, to show that you have passed from darkness to light,

Shine as a light in the world to the glory of God;

God has received you by baptism into his Church

We welcome you into the Lord's family.

The Church teaches

Baptism is a true sacrament instituted by Christ. It is administered by washing with natural water and [calling upon] the most Holy Trinity. Anybody … can validly administer baptism. It confers grace by signs … so children should be baptized while still infants. Baptism is necessary for salvation. It causes the remission of original and actual sins and all punishments due to sin. It confers grace,

membership in Christ and in the Church and the obligation to obey the Church's laws. (From study guide, Hexham diocese.)

Believers' baptism

As the term implies, the people make up their own minds to be baptized in public, to make a statement of faith. The Baptist Church got its name from the fact that they baptized believers, other denominations are the Pentecostals and the Brethren Church. Some Anglican churches baptize older candidates by full immersion if requested.

Why wait?

Many Christians will say that it is unfair to impose something on a child they might dislike later on. Baptists say that the candidates must understand what they are undertaking. The candidates must make the choice to follow Jesus or not, learn about their commitment and their role in the life of the Church.

Once baptized, they may take a full part in the life of the church. When the person is immersed under the water and then comes up again it symbolizes dying to an old life and coming alive again in a new life with Christ.

Order of service

- Candidates will have attended a group beforehand for basic guidance and teaching.

- The service begins with hymns, general prayers and bible readings.

- Before the person enters the pool, he may be asked to give a **testimony** (arranged beforehand), where he recounts how he came to this decision.

- Some churches ask questions about basic beliefs and then ask, 'Do you accept Jesus as Lord and Saviour?'

- The candidate is led into the pool and pulled forward or back under the water. The minister says, '*I baptize you in the name of the Father, Son and Holy Spirit*'.

- The candidate is filled with the Holy Spirit and leaves the pool.

- Holy Communion often follows.

Confirmation

Confirmation is the completion of baptism. It is the sign of maturity, sometimes called 'coming of age'. The baby is now a teenager or an adult and professes their Christian faith for themselves.

Who confirms?

The bishop always confirms as he performs the laying on of hands.

What age?

The age varies. Many Roman Catholic churches in England will only confirm teenagers upwards, when they truly make up their own minds. This is true of the Anglican Church as well. They try to ensure that there is no undue parental pressure. In some places, the Roman Catholic Church will confirm from eleven and some from seven.

Why confirmation?

People seek confirmation for varying reasons.

- The teenager or adult may want to strengthen their faith. They are regular church-goers and, for the teenagers, it will also symbolize that they are grown-up independent beings.
- It shows that the person is now taking the decision for himself.
- For many adults it may follow on straight from being baptized and is a declaration of belief (they were not baptized as babies).
- For some adults, confirmation is a public display that they have changed their lives, 'turned over a new leaf', they now follow Jesus Christ.

Getting ready

The number of teaching sessions will depend on the priest, the church and those being confirmed. If there is a large contingent of teenagers being confirmed, it is often usual for them to have their own sessions. If the church has a youth leader, they may take them.

These are some of the topics for teaching:

- basic Roman Catholic beliefs about baptism, the Bible, life after death, the seven sacraments
- the meaning of baptism and confirmation
- the Bible
- prayer and worship
- the Holy Spirit.

Order of Roman Catholic service

This usually takes place in a Eucharistic service. The order is followed until confirmation.

- Bible readings, usually about the Holy Spirit.
- The priest asks the candidates to stand.
- The bishop briefly summarizes the meaning of confirmation.
- The candidates answer five questions/promises that were made for them at baptism:
    1. Do you reject Satan?
    2. Do you believe in God the Father?
    3. Do you believe in Jesus his only Son, born of Virgin Mary, crucified, died, buried, and rose from the dead, now seated with God?
    4. Do you believe in the Holy Spirit?
    5. Do you believe in the holy, catholic church … and the life everlasting?
- The candidates reply, 'I do'.
- The bishop prays for all the candidates to receive the Holy Spirit.

- Each candidate kneels in front of the bishop, accompanied by their sponsor. The sponsor puts their hand on the candidate's shoulder.
- The bishop puts his right hand on the person's head, makes the sign of the cross with chrism on the forehead and says, 'Be sealed with the gift of the Holy Spirit. Peace be with you.' Then they shake hands.
- The Eucharist continues.

Laying on of hands

This is an ancient sign and symbolizes the coming down and the entering of a person by the Holy Spirit, full of power and courage.

Anointing with chrism

Again, this is an ancient sign meaning you are made special (for example, David was anointed to be King of Israel). It also symbolizes the Holy Spirit being sealed into the person and the idea of healing. You begin a new life, healed of past sins.

Personal effects of confirmation

- The person receives the Holy Spirit.
- Once an adult, the person has full rights within the parish and may hold office.
- He/she should aim to mature and get closer to God.
- He/she should want to be more like Christ, for example, through prayer.

- He/she should strive to obey Jesus.
- He/she must share their beliefs with others.
- He/she should read the Bible, attend church regularly, get involved and go to confession.
- Some priests say that others should notice a difference in their lives.

The Church teaches

Confirmation is a true sacrament instituted by Christ and different from baptism. It is administered by laying on of hands and anointing with chrism, accompanied by prayer. The chrism is blessed by the bishop who gives the sacrament. All baptized persons can and should be confirmed. The effect of the sacrament of confirmation is to give strength in faith and to impress an indelible character. (From study guide, Hexham diocese.)

Activities

1 Role play. Three in a group: priest, mum and dad. Imagine that mum and dad come to see the priest to arrange the baptism of three month old daughter Jade. Dad is less keen on baptism than mum (he does not go to church that much) and he wants Jade really to decide for herself. Act out the scene as the priest gives advice. By the end of the scene, did they arrange a date for baptism or not? Practise and then watch each group perform. You could video it. **WO 2.1, 2.2, 2.3**

2 If you were the priest, would you agree to baptize Jade or not? Give reasons. **C 2.1a**

Key points

- The issue of baptism is complicated with many different views.
- Baptism is initiation into the Church.
- Some parents decide to leave it up to their children to decide when they are older.

The Eucharist

Different denominations call the celebration of the Last Supper by different names depending on their focus or emphasis.

- Eucharist – celebrated by the Anglican and Roman Catholic churches for praise, worship and thanksgiving.
- **Mass** – celebrated by the Roman Catholic Church as a set ritual to celebrate the Eucharist, emphasizing the sacrifice of Jesus on the cross.
- **Holy Communion** – celebrated by many churches for closeness to God and being together.
- Liturgy – celebrated by the Orthodox Church as a set form of service in public, an offering to God.
- Lord's Supper – celebrated by the Baptist and Pentecostal churches by doing exactly what Jesus said.
- Breaking of Bread – celebrated by the Brethren Church for sharing together. It is often regarded as a meal.

The most common name in the Roman Catholic Church is the Mass. The word Mass comes from the Latin *missa* meaning 'sent'. It was taken from the end of the Eucharist where the congregation is sent out into the world. *Ite, misse est*, literally meaning 'Go the Eucharist has been sent'. Today the words said by the priest are: 'Go in peace, to love and serve the Lord.'

The early church

Christian communities up to the end of the fourth century, celebrated the Eucharist in groups in a home. They would incorporate the Eucharist into a meal (sometimes called agape meal or friendship meal).

Paul wrote to some of the early churches because he was concerned that many Christians were getting drunk at these celebrations and not sharing!

Later changes

The ritual has evolved in many ways, such as the change from Latin to the language of the people, different names and the importance placed on its celebration. The Eucharist is most often celebrated in a church or a chapel. Musical settings of the Mass often brought fame. J. S. Bach composed his *B minor Mass*, a work of difficulty. Haydn and Mozart wrote many settings, but only a few survive, such as *The Nelson Mass*. Victorian composers, such as Stanford and Darke, composed simpler settings for general choir use. In the twentieth century, Richard Sheppherd and Rawsthorne's settings became popular.

Why is the Eucharist important for Christians?

- The Eucharist remembers and re-enacts the Last Supper, during which Jesus himself said, 'Do this to remember me.'
- Some denominations, such as the Baptists and Methodists, only celebrate the Eucharist once a month in the morning and once in the evening (except for special festivals). They believe that explaining God's word in sermons is just as important and need time to study in depth.
- Many Christians believe that Jesus is with them in a special way in this service, giving them renewed strength.

The bread and wine

- Denominations, such as Roman Catholics and the Orthodox Church, believe that the living, risen Jesus is actually present in the bread and wine, so when they eat bread and drink wine they receive Jesus into themselves in a personal way.

- Others, like Methodists, Baptists and Anglicans believe that the bread and wine do not change spiritually or physically, they remain bread and wine. They are symbols of Jesus' body and blood. Jesus is present in every part of the service.

Roman Catholic order of service

Introduction and penitence

- After a hymn and welcome the congregation confesses their sins to be right with God.

- Kyrie (Lord/Christ have mercy) and Gloria (praise).

Liturgy of the Word

- Bible readings.
- Homily (sermon) explaining God's Word.
- **Nicene creed** (beliefs of Christians).
- Prayer for others and ourselves.

Liturgy of the Eucharist

- Bread, wine and the collection brought to the altar. The **celebrant** thanks God and begins the Eucharistic prayer.

- Celebrant repeats the words of Jesus: 'This is my body broken for you. This is the cup of my blood … it will be shed for you'. The bread and wine become Jesus' body and blood.

- Lord's prayer.

- The Peace, people greet each other saying, 'Peace be with you'.

- People move to the altar to receive the bread (the host), 'the body of Christ'.

- In many Roman Catholic churches **communicant**s also receive wine. In the Orthodox Church, bread is dipped in wine and offered on a spoon.

- 'Go in peace to love and serve the Lord'.

In the Roman Catholic Church only an ordained priest (who may be a bishop) may celebrate the Eucharist.

He is called the celebrant. The bread used is usually a special wafer.

The Church teaches

The Holy Eucharist is a true sacrament instituted by Christ himself. Christ is really present in the Eucharist, even when not being received. It is to be honoured and adored, the whole of Christ is present in either kind (bread and wine) and is received by the communicant. The bread and wine are 'transubstantiated' by the priest into the flesh and blood of Christ, only the appearance of the bread and wine remains.

Holy Mass is a sacrifice instituted by Christ at the Last Supper; it represents his sacrifice on the cross …In every liturgical activity Christ is present. (From study guide, Hexham diocese.)

Activities

1. Some denominations celebrate communion every Sunday, others less so. They might say that explaining God's Word is more important.

   a What are the disadvantages of always having the Eucharist as the main service every Sunday?

   a Why do you think some churches think explaining God's Word is more important? **C 1.1, 2.1a, IT 1.1, 2.2**

2. Have a agape meal as a class (bring and share). Your local Pentecostal church may help. **IT 2.2, WO 2.1, 2.2**

3. Research the Passover meal. How is it different from Communion? What changes did Jesus make? You could invite a leader from a church to talk to you about their way of doing things. **IT 2.1**

Key points

- There are many names for the Eucharist and just as many ways of celebrating it.
- Most denominations require you to be a member in order to take communion.

Bible passages

In this section there are some useful passages that you can use in your answers.

Matthew 28: 18–20 (The commission)

> Then Jesus came to them and said, 'All authority in heaven and on earth has been given to me. Therefore go and make disciples of all nations, baptizing them in the name of the Father and of the Son and of the Holy Spirit, and teaching them to obey everything I have commanded you. And surely I am with you always, to the very end of the age.'

Jesus is regarded as instituting the baptism of believers – first you preach the gospel, then baptize those who believe.

Acts 2: 37, 38 and 41–7 (Response)

> When the people heard this, they were cut to the heart and said to Peter and the other apostles, 'Brothers, what shall we do?' Peter replied, 'Repent and be baptized, every one of you, in the name of Jesus Christ for the forgiveness of your sins. And you will receive the gift of the Holy Spirit.'
>
> Those who accepted his message were baptized, and about three thousand were added to their number that day. They devoted themselves to the apostles' teaching and to the fellowship, to the breaking of bread and to prayer. Everyone was filled with awe, and many wonders and miraculous signs were done by the apostles.
>
> All the believers were together and had everything in common. Selling their possessions and goods, they gave to anyone as he had need. Every day they continued to meet together in the temple courts. They broke bread in their homes and ate together with glad and sincere hearts, praising God and enjoying the favour of all the people. And the Lord added to their number daily those who were being saved.

The obvious response when people turn to Christ is to be baptized as a public sign.

Acts 8: 34–9 (Story of baptism)

> The eunuch asked Philip, 'Tell me, please, who is the prophet talking about, himself or someone else?' Then Philip began with that very passage of Scripture and told him the good news about Jesus. As they travelled along the road, they came to some water and the eunuch said, 'Look, here is water. Why shouldn't I be baptized?' And he gave orders to stop the chariot. Then both Philip and the eunuch went down into the water and Philip baptized him. When they came up out of the water, the Spirit of the Lord suddenly took Philip away, and the eunuch did not see him again, but went on his way rejoicing.

The full story is in verses 26–40. Here baptism was spontaneous, there were no preparation classes. It was a public declaration of faith.

1 Corinthians 11: 17–34

> In the following directives I have no praise for you, for your meetings do more harm than good. In the first place, I hear that when you come together as a church, there are divisions among you, and to some extent I believe it. No doubt there have to be differences among you

to show which of you have God's approval. When you come together, it is not the Lord's Supper you eat, for as you eat, each of you goes ahead without waiting for anybody else. One remains hungry, another gets drunk. Don't you have homes to eat and drink in? Or do you despise the church of God and humiliate those who have nothing? What shall I say to you? Shall I praise you for this? Certainly not!

For I received from the Lord what I also passed on to you: The Lord Jesus, on the night he was betrayed, took bread, and when he had given thanks, he broke it and said, 'This is my body, which is for you; do this in remembrance of me.' In the same way, after supper he took the cup, saying, 'This cup is the new covenant in my blood; do this, whenever you drink it, in remembrance of me.' For whenever you eat this bread and drink this cup, you proclaim the Lord's death until he comes.

Therefore, whoever eats the bread or drinks the cup of the Lord in an unworthy manner will be guilty of sinning against the body and blood of the Lord. A man ought to examine himself before he eats of the bread and drinks of the cup. For anyone who eats and drinks without recognizing the body of the Lord eats and drinks judgement on himself. That is why many among you are weak and sick, and a number of you have fallen asleep. But if we judged ourselves, we would not come under judgement. When we are judged by the Lord, we are being disciplined so that we will not be condemned with the world.

So then, my brothers, when you come together to eat, wait for each other. If anyone is hungry, he should eat at home, so that when you meet together it may not result in judgement. And when I come I will give further directions.

Paul is in fact reprimanding the church in Corinth and thus gives a unique insight into early church worship. It would appear that they have forgotten they are all equal and some get more than others. The church has turned the ceremony into a meal (this was normal practice in the early church), an agape followed by communion. The meal was supposed to be a sharing meal, but this clearly was not happening – some began before others, some got more than their fair share, some even got drunk. There was no evidence of Christian values. Then Paul gives 'an order of service' still used today. Finally, he points out that taking communion is serious and should not be taken lightly and should only be received in the right frame of mind.

Activities

1 Try and learn some of these passages so that you can use them to support your answers in exams. **PS 2.1**

2 Do you think that it is going against the Bible to baptize children and have private ceremonies? Give reasons. **C 1.1, 2.1a**

3 Try and find out if your church/some churches near you are having/have had an agape meal. Find out what happens and why they do it. **IT 2.1, PS 2.2**

Exam questions to practise

Below are some sample exam questions for paper 2B. To help you score full marks, the first three questions are followed by some tips from examiners. Before attempting the remaining two questions, try to work out your own strategy for approaching them.

1 Explain why a candle is used in baptism. (2)

2 Explain the meaning of the following in the sacrament of confirmation:
   a laying on of hands
   b anointing with chrism. (4)

3 Explain what Jesus said about the bread and the wine in his last meal with his disciples. (4)

Now try questions 4 and 5 on your own. Before you write your answers, spend some time thinking about your approach.

4 'Being confirmed makes you into a better Christian.' Do you agree? Give reasons for your answer, showing you have thought about more than one point of view. (5)

5

> 'I tell you the truth, whatever you did for one of the least of these brothers of mine, you did it for me.' *(The Parable of the Sheep and the Goats)*

A

> 'Give a man a fish and you feed him for a day; teach him to fish and you feed him for life.' *(A phrase to explain the work of CAFOD/ Trócaire)*

B

> 'Go in peace to love and serve the Lord.' *(The last words of the Mass)*

C

   a Explain how the words in box **A** are related to the words in box **C**. (3)
   b Explain how the words in box **B** are related to the words in box **C**. (3)

How to score full marks

1 Do not write too much, as it is only worth 2 marks. The mark scheme will probably say: One reason given = 1 mark. One reason explained = 1 mark.

2 This will be marked 2 + 2. Do not write too much. Think of why the bishop does these two things.

3 This will probably be 2 marks for the bread and 2 marks for the wine. Think about what Jesus said and what it meant.

Personal issues relating to the sacraments 2

This section includes:

- Why get married?
- The wedding ceremony
- When things go wrong
- Churches' attitudes to divorce and remarriage
- Sex before marriage
- What is abortion?
- Views for and against abortion
- Bible passages
- Exam questions to practise

This section considers the concept of Christian marriage from the viewpoints of different churches. It looks at the effects of the wedding vows on the rest of the couple's lives, but recognizes that sometimes relationships go wrong and may end in divorce. Abortion is discussed as part of this section. It is acknowledged that it is a very emotive subject and thus is handled with care. There are alternative viewpoints put forward.

Why get married?

Key terms

Marriage Being married.

Vows Solemn promises, in the wedding ceremony between husband and wife.

Wedding The marriage service.

Marriage: fairytale or reality?

Getting married! Some magazines say it is a girl's dream: engagement ring, fairy-tale **wedding**, expensive dress, gifts, honeymoon, hunk of a husband. For the man it could mean a gorgeous wife who he can show off and who will take care of all his needs. Happy ever after?

Not long ago, in 1981, this scenario was played out on television and in the newspapers. Indeed, the whole world knows the story of Prince Charles and Lady Diana. It is a fact that 81 per cent of adults in the UK will marry at some time in their lives and nearly half will divorce. Yet people continue to get married and Christians teach that **marriage** is a good thing – the only really suitable environment for children.

A Christian marriage

The Church of England 2000 Book of Common Worship has an excellent introduction to the wedding service that sums up the Christian purpose of marriage (see opposite).

Christian purpose of marriage

In the presence of God, Father Son and Holy Spirit.

We have come together to witness the marriage of [name] and [name].

To pray for God's blessing on them, to share their joy and celebrate love.

Marriage is the gift of God in creation.

It is given that as man and woman grow together in love and trust,

They shall be united with one another, in heart, body and mind,

As Christ is united with his bride the Church.

The gift of marriage brings husband and wife together in the delight and tenderness of sexual union and joyful commitment to the end of their lives.

It is given as the foundation of family life in which children are [born and] nurtured and in which each member of the family, in good times and bad, may find strength, companionship and comfort, and grow to maturity in love.

Marriage is a way of life made holy by God and blessed by the presence of our Lord Jesus Christ …

Marriage is a sign of unity and loyalty which all should uphold and honour; it enriches society and strengthens community.

No one should enter into it lightly or selfishly, but reverently and responsibly in the sight of almighty God.

[Name] and [name] are now to enter this way of life; they will give their consent to the other and make solemn **vows** and in token of this they will give and receive rings.

We pray with them that the Holy Spirit will guide them, that they may fulfil God's purposes for the whole of their earthly life together.

A Christian wedding takes place in front of God as a witness and with all the couple's friends to share in their joy.

Marriage is seen as the right place for making love, a sign of commitment, and the unit into which children are born and raised. Families provide back-up in good times and bad. It is seen as a good thing for society and Jesus backed this ideal. The couple are reminded that marriage should not be taken lightly. They are to make solemn vows and give rings.

Can you marry anyone?

In the UK if someone is already married he or she cannot marry again until divorced or the death of his or her spouse. There are also certain other prohibitions by law.

Who cannot get married

Marriage between a person and any of the following relatives is totally prohibited:

- parent
- child
- adopted child
- grandparent
- grandchild
- sibling (brother or sister)
- aunt or uncle
- niece or nephew.

The rules about weddings in a Roman Catholic Church

The Roman Catholic Church follows UK law, which requires weddings to take place between 8am and 6pm (except by special licence, normally only for medical emergency). The service must be in English (Welsh is allowed in Wales).

In the Roman Catholic Church, marriage is usually by 'common licence'. One of the couple must have lived in the parish where the marriage is to take place for a minimum of fifteen days. Many Roman Catholic Churches will not have weddings during Lent and certainly not on Maundy Thursday, Good Friday and Easter Saturday.

Couples who marry abroad, either because one of them originated there or because they want a 'marriage package', including the wedding on a beach, are warned to check that the marriage will be legal in the eyes of British law. There have been cases of couples married on a far away beach and finding out later that they are not legally married.

Will there be problems in a mixed marriage?

A mixed marriage in Britain is usually regarded as meaning that the husband and wife belong to different religions or races – for example, the man is Muslim and the woman is Christian. Some of these marriages work well with few or no problems, but some face many difficulties. Some couples do not realize the problems until they are already married. Consider the problems of a Christian/Muslim couple below:

- The first problem may be where to get married – in a mosque, in a church or in a Register Office?
- If the couple has children, which religion will they be brought up in? Muslim or Christian? Will they be given Muslim or Christian names? When the children are older, will they worship in a mosque or a church?

Activities

1 Look at the Christian purpose of marriage. Which purpose do you think is most important? Give reasons. **PS 2.1**

2 Consider two problems that mixed marriages can face.
   a For each problem work out a possible solution. (Work in groups, with each group in turn telling the whole class the solutions they have thought of.)
   b Try to list any other problems the couple may face. **C 2.1b, WO 2.2**

Key points

- Marriage is regarded as a life-long, serious commitment.
- Marriage is regarded by Christians of all denominations as the context within which to have sex and to raise children.

The wedding ceremony

One of the most important parts of the wedding service is the point when the couple make their vows. Although the wording may differ slightly, the vows basically mean the same thing. The key word to sum up the vows is **commitment**.

The priest begins by asking questions:

- Are you freely and without reservation ready to give yourselves to each other in marriage?
- Are you ready to love and honour each other as man and wife for the rest of your life?
- Are you ready to accept children lovingly from God and bring them up according to the law of Christ and his Church?

The couple then declare that they know of no reason (in law) why they should not get married. Then they each say that they freely wish to marry and that no one is forcing them to do so.

Order of Service

The order of service outlined below is from the Roman Catholic Church.

Entry	The Bride, her father (or other male relative) and her attendants process to the front of the church. The bridegroom stands on her right.
Hymn	The congregation sings.
Welcome	From the priest.
Reading	From the Bible. One chosen by the couple, a psalm and then one from a gospel.
Talk	By the priest.
Vows	First the priest questions the couple (see above), then the couple make promises to each other in front of God and their friends in church.
Exchange of rings	It is common practice these days for both husband and wife to exchange rings.
Proclamation	The couple are now married – husband and wife!
Blessing	A reminder that nobody should break the bond made before God.
Prayers	Asking God to help and bless the couple in the many aspects and roles of marriage.
Nuptial Mass	If the couple wish to receive communion.
Hymn(s)	The congregation sings.
Nuptial blessing	
Registration	The couple sign the Register of Marriages (one will be stored in London, one kept by the church records and one for the couple). A minimum of two other witnesses and the vicar also sign the register.
Hymn	The congregation sings.
The couple leave	The couple leave the church, followed by their friends and relatives.

Vows made during the wedding ceremony

1 I call upon these people present to witness that I, *Name*, do take you, *Name*,
2 To be my lawful wedded husband/wife,
3 To have and to hold from this day forward,
4 For better, for worse,
5 For richer, for poorer,
6 In sickness and in health,
7 To love and to cherish
8 'Til death us do part.

There are basic meanings to the vows with the underlying concept of commitment to each other.

1 The friends and family witness the couple's promises.
2 The marriage will be legal in the eyes of your country. The words 'take you' is left over from the old idea that when a woman got married everything became her husband's; he literally took everything, including land, titles and money, so she became totally dependent on him.
3 They have each other.
4 The couple will stay together in the bad times as well as the good, when it is easier for a marriage to work, for example, when one of them is depressed due to losing their job, they will stick together and support each other.
5 In days when the budget is tight, they still find fun together. The couple do not split up because they cannot buy what they please.
6 It is easier for marriage when you are both well, but when one is ill and does not want sex, it can put a strain on things, as can when you find out your spouse is infertile. But this is no excuse to leave. When one of the couple is ill, it can bring them closer together. The important thing is to be there for each other as a shoulder to cry on!
7 Both partners will love each other, care for each other and respect each other.
8 Marriage is for life.

Rings are given and the couple say, 'Take this ring as a sign of my love and **fidelity** (faithfulness)'.

Marriage is a sacrament

Roman Catholics and many other Christians believe that marriage is a **sacrament**. A sacrament is a ceremony or ritual through which Christians come to know God better. It is an outward sign of an inward blessing from God. God works to bring people closer to him. In marriage each partner becomes the channel of God's love to the other. God is present when the vows are made and a sacramental bond is created, which persists regardless of what happens to the human relationship itself. Other Christians would disagree saying that the vows are 'declarations of intent', they are made in all seriousness with the intention of keeping them, but they allow for situations when the vows cannot be kept any more. In 1985 the **Catechism** reiterated:

'Marriage is the sacrament in which baptized men and women vow to belong to each other in a permanent and exclusive sexual partnership of loving mutual care, concern and shared responsibility, in the hope of having children and bringing up a family.' *(Printed by the Catholic Truth Society.)*

Activities

1 Make up a set of vows that you would have at your wedding. Read your list to the person next to you, then explain why you have chosen these vows. **C 1.3, WO 2.2**
2 Do you agree that a couple should be able to marry anywhere these days – such as in castles, on a beach? Give reasons. This can be done in groups. **C 2.1a**

Key points

- Whatever the denomination, there are similar key parts in the Christian service.
- The most important part is the sharing of the vows, which are similar whichever church a couple might go to.
- The vows are serious, made in front of God, the couple's witness.

When things go wrong

Key terms

Adultery Where two people have sex by consent, but one or both of them are already married to someone else. It is sometimes called 'having an affair' or 'extra-marital sex'.

Divorce The legal termination of a marriage, leaving the couple free to remarry who they like.

Marriages do not always last forever.

Before the twentieth century **divorce** was rare. A woman who was divorced was usually alone in the world – she lost everything and there was rarely a divorce settlement. However, over the last 100 years or so, there have been gradual reforms in the law.

Law reform in marriage

- *1971 Divorce Reform Act.* A divorce could be granted on the grounds of adultery, cruelty, desertion of more than two years by one of the couple, or by mutual agreement after two years (after five if one partner did not want a divorce). A husband or a wife could initiate proceedings.

- *1984 Matrimonial and Family Proceedings Act.* Divorce was allowed after a minimum of one year.

- *1995 White Paper.* Couples were encouraged to seek mediation or counselling before divorce. 'Proving fault' was removed and couples were encouraged to reach their own settlements, approved in court.

- *1998 Government Guidelines for Newly Weds.* One suggestion here was a network of marriage preparation classes, videos about marriage and advice on things like bank accounts.

When Christians might accept divorce

In the case of domestic violence, some Christians would say it is better for the abused and the children, if there are any, to leave and to start a new life. The abused spouse might be killed next time.

Many Christians quote what Jesus said in Matthew 5: 27–32 (see page 126) – that is, divorce is wrong except in cases of **adultery**.

Some quote a passage from 1 Corinthians 7. Paul said that if a Christian is married to an unbeliever who then walks out due to the other's Christian beliefs, they are not bound in marriage. They believe it is still God's word and that it is still applicable in the twenty-first century.

People are only human and should be given second chances. They might have made a mistake, but why should they pay for it forever?

Why couples get divorced

There are many reasons why couples get divorced, as this diagram shows.

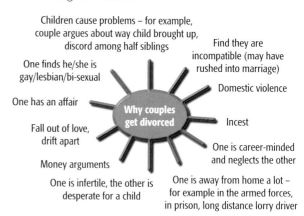

When Christians are against divorce

In Mark 10 (see page 126), Jesus said that divorce was wrong under any circumstances. He built on Malachi, where God said, 'I hate divorce.'

Christians regard marriage as a life-long commitment, with promises made in front of God. Those who regard marriage as a sacrament say that it cannot be ended, only by God.

We live in a society where everything has to be instant. A marriage has to be worked at and will take time. There are likely to be 'rocky' periods in the marriage, but working through these should strengthen the couple's relationship.

Many people think divorce is too quick and easy. Many couples ignore advice to get mediation and help. If there are children, the effect of divorce must be considered.

Where couples can seek advice

There are a number of places where couples can seek help in times of crisis.

Marriage Care

This service (previously known as the Catholic Marriage Advisory Council), was relaunched by the Roman Catholic Church in 2000. It was renamed for two reasons:

1 Research showed the old name was off-putting, potentially excluding other Christians. Today, Marriage Care has 73 centres for the whole community, not just Roman Catholics.

2 Marriage Care now emphasizes its expertize at working with married couples. It recognizes the effects of divorce and separation on the whole family.

Marriage Care wanted to show compassion to those couples in difficulty – not disapproval and reminders of strict Church teaching. It stresses that only the couples themselves can save their marriages. Additionally, it runs marriage preparation classes for couples getting married.

Relate

The Relate website introduces itself by stating it provides counselling, sex therapy, relationship education and training to support couples and families. At present there are over 2,500 counsellors in Britain and the service remains independent, free of any government control. Relate will help any adult who is having relationship problems. Relate is non-religious, but many Christians use Relate or work for it. Some of its services include couple counselling, mediation, or counselling for teenagers whose parents have separated or divorced.

CARE (Christian Action Research and Education)

This is supported by many denominations, especially **evangelical churches** and the Free Church movement. It aims to demonstrate Jesus' compassion and emphasize the family. It writes resources and briefing packs and gets involved in public policy. It organizes courses, such as 'Talking to your children', and 'Talking to your spouse', and provides resources for schools and churches.

Activities

1 'Adultery is OK so long as you don't get caught.' Do you agree? **C 2.1a**

2 Why do you think people have affairs? Make a list of reasons. **PS 2.1**

3 Act out the following role play. You will need three people – the marriage counsellor (male or female), the wife and the husband.

The couple always seem to be arguing and criticizing each other. They do not go out together, the wife has headaches, the husband says he does not like his wife's clothes, the wife says she does not like his friends and so on. The wife has 'dragged' her husband to see the counsellor. This is the first session.

Act out the therapy session, which you can make serious or humorous. Practise and perform to the rest of the class.

C2.1b, WO 2.3

Key points

- Marriages are meant for life, but sadly some just do not work out.
- One key reason for divorce is abuse of the partner – domestic violence.
- Some Christians are against divorce on *any* grounds.
- There are many agencies that provide counselling.

Churches' attitudes to divorce and remarriage

Attitudes to divorce

Annulment

The Roman Catholic Church does not recognize divorce – once married the vows cannot be ended, they are there for life until death. The Church will grant **annulments**, which say the marriage did not happen, it is null and void. There are several reasons, such as:

- One of the couple did not understand the vows.
- One or both of the couple were forced to marry.
- One of them never intended to have a child (no medical problem/infertility).
- The marriage was not **consummated** (no sex).
- One or both never intended to remain faithful.
- Lies, for example, one spouse lied that they were not infertile.
- Incest.
- Concealment, for example, it is found out that one is an alcoholic.

A marriage tribunal will consider each case, but the 'accused' spouse does not have to co-operate. Most tribunals require three witnesses to support the allegations. Annulments are often turned down. Children born in a marriage later annulled, are declared legitimate.

Catechism 2385 says: 'Divorce is immoral because it introduces disorder into the family and into society.' It ends: 'Because of its contagious effect [it is] truly a plague on society.'

- In principle, the *Church of England* does not accept divorce and follows Jesus' words in Matthew 5. The Church teaches that marriage is for life. It states that when the vows are taken the couple should fully intend to keep them. This is called 'declaration of intent'. But it accepts there may be circumstances when the vows cannot be kept. The Church prays for forgiveness and renewal in a marriage while acknowledging that for some there will be divorce and **remarriage**.

- Some *Free churches* say it is not the death of one of the spouses that ends a marriage, it is the death of love between the couple. So it is better to divorce than live a lie. They say that God is 'open to the future' and the church should respond with flexibility.

Attitudes to remarriage

Divorced people often meet someone and want to marry again. The problem for them is that many Churches will not marry divorcees.

- The *Church of England* accepts that divorce happens for valid reasons. Vicars legally should not remarry divorced people in church but can offer a Service of Blessing after the Register Office wedding. Individual churches draw up their own policy. One church near Chester did this. The policy stated:

There will be a period of three months' cooling down from when the vicar is asked. After three months, there will be a meeting at which the vicar will ask questions about the previous marriage(s) and the reasons for divorce. Then the church wardens will be invited to a second meeting. If the vicar is happy that maturity is shown, there are no ongoing court proceedings, such as child access, animosity with the former spouse(s) is not evident and the couple have the right attitude to their own relationship, then preparations can begin. It is to be made clear that one or both of them must be a regular attender at this church.

- The *Roman Catholic Church* will not remarry couples as it does not accept divorce. There is no Service of Blessing. The original vows were made for life and a sacramental bond has been made that cannot be broken, so a legal divorce is not recognized. If a person remarries, the couple commit adultery because in the eyes of the church the original marriage still stands.

Catechism 1650 says: 'If the divorced are remarried civilly they find themselves in a situation which contravenes God's law. Consequently they cannot receive [Holy] Communion as long as this situation persists.'

Catechism 2384 says: 'Contracting a new union, even if it is recognized by civil law, adds to the [seriousness of the situation]; the remarried spouse is then in a situation of permanent adultery. If a husband, separated from his wife, approaches another woman, he is an adulterer because he makes that woman commit adultery also.'

Status of divorced people in the Roman Catholic Church

Roman Catholics do get divorced, although they are still married in the eyes of the Church. A divorced person may receive Holy Communion and when they die may be buried in a Roman Catholic cemetery after the Requiem Mass. In May 1977, it was announced that the penalty of excommunication would be lifted, it does not apply to divorced or remarried people. The church recognizes that some divorcees cannot get an annulment and choose to live a single life, held in high esteem, and backed by the teaching of St Paul. There are chances to help others, go abroad to help agencies or work in inner cities without the worry of thinking about your family.

In a Roman Catholic wedding, vows are made for life.

Activities

1 Imagine you are a Roman Catholic or Church of England priest/vicar. A couple want to be married in your church but one of them is divorced. They live in the parish and sometimes go to church. Working in pairs or small groups discuss the following questions.
   a How would you justify your refusal to marry them in church?
   b What advice would you give them?
   c What would the couple say in their defence? **C 2.1a, WO 2.3**

2 If you were allowed to marry the couple in church, would you? Give reasons. **PS 2.1, 2.3**

3 'Annulment is just another word for divorce.' Do you agree with this statement? Make a list of points for and against. **PS 2.1, 2.3**

Key points

- The Roman Catholic Church does not recognize divorce, so there is no question of remarriage.
- The Church of England does accept there may be situations where there will be divorce.
- There are churches that will remarry people in the hope they will start to attend their services regularly.

Sex before marriage

The 1960s were seen by many as a period of sexual freedom.

There has always been a debate about sex before marriage – right or wrong? When people research their family histories, it seems there are often cases of children born soon after the wedding or with a different surname. With the advent of the Pill, more people felt safe enough in the 1960s and 70s to chance one-night stands. The idea was to have fun. The AIDS scare of the 1980s gradually led people to accept that using condoms could prevent the spread of disease.

What the churches say

- The Roman Catholic Church is clear on its teaching about sex before marriage – also called **fornication**. Catechism 2353 says: 'Fornication is sensual union between an unmarried man and woman. It is gravely against the dignity of the persons and of sexuality which is naturally ordered for the good of married couples and the [conception and raising] of children.'
- Some members of the *Church of England* say it has been too lax over its teaching about sex before marriage. In 1995 a report called 'Something to celebrate' was published. It was about family life and reaffirmed the Christian belief that marriage provided the proper context for sexual relationships.

Living together

Living together is still a controversial issue in the twenty-first century.

Is living together right …?

- Marriage is a piece of paper. You can make your own commitment to each other, without the need for a wedding certificate.
- Marriage can be costly, especially if you go for 'the full works' – a huge white wedding, big reception and exotic honeymoon.
- It is a good trial for marriage to see if you get on with each other when living as a couple.
- A lot of people, including some Christians, say the divorce rate is high and rising, so it might be better to have a trial marriage. They might say that if you bought an expensive car you would test drive it first!

… or is living together wrong?

- The Roman Catholic Church uses the same arguments as the ones against sex before marriage.
- In 1992 the Church of England produced a report called 'Cohabitation: a Background Paper'. It said that while it was accepted that people live together, 'the [Church of England] is concerned to sustain the institution of marriage and the family'.

  The report recognizes that there are many reasons for living together, such as being wary of commitment after an abusive marriage. It encourages couples to make a public stand that they are living as man and wife by making promises before God and their friends.
- If you live together there is no real commitment. It is easier to get out of the relationship so there is no incentive to make the relationship work.
- Many of the older generations say that if you get pregnant the mother will be 'an unmarried mother' and the child branded 'illegitimate'.

- Living together is often called 'living in sin'. Christians believe sex is no longer special if you do not wait until marriage, and that every act of love should include the possibility of creating a new life. Most Christians believe that the only suitable place to bring up a child is within marriage.

- Because Christians, such as Roman Catholics, regard marriage as a sacrament, they believe that God is with them, binding them together. The Roman Catholic catechism states 'a man and woman belong to each other in a permanent, exclusive, sexual partnership'. This cannot happen until commitment is made through the wedding vows.

Should you wait to have sex?

Many teenagers feel great pressure to have a boyfriend or girlfriend, to start dating and then have sex as quickly as possible.

In the USA some (mainly Christian) teenagers began to rebel against a culture in which they felt sex was not regarded as special. You were regarded as 'odd' or a 'freak' if you were still a virgin at sixteen. Men added women to their lists of conquests and wanted to marry 'experienced women'. Men expected women to control contraception and to agree to sex if asked.

The teenagers met on the Internet and called themselves True Love Waits. A True Love Waits group was founded in Nashville in 1995, supported by the local church. The church designed a special ceremony whereby the child promises not to have sex until marriage. A pledge card is signed and a ring given as these words are spoken: 'Let this ring be a constant reminder to you to be sexually pure'. Children who take part in this are both male and female and are usually about the age of twelve or over.

There is concern from other Christian groups that there is parental pressure to take the pledge and that the group is quite extremist. They question how a child of twelve can really know whether he or she will not want sex until marriage. How can anyone know their opinions of the future or what the future holds?

True Love Waits
Believing that true love waits,
I make a commitment to God, myself,
My family, my future partner,
And my future children,
To be sexually pure until the day
I enter into a covenant marriage relationship.

Signed:_____

Activities

1 Do you think people are making a fuss about nothing about living together? Discuss in groups of two or three.
   C 2.1a, PS 2.1, WO 2.3

2 Act out the following role play. One of you is a seventeen-year-old, planning to move out of home to live with your partner. The other one/two are mum and dad.

   Your parent(s) disagree with sex before marriage and living together. Act out the conversation that takes place when you tell them you are moving out. Then perform your role play to the whole class.
   C 2.1b, WO 2.3

3 Re-read the passage on True Love Waits. In groups answer the following questions.
   a Why did the teenagers form their group?
   b Are the pressures for sex the same in the UK or different? Give reasons.
   c What did you think first when you read the pledge?
   d Why are some people concerned about True Love Waits?
   e Would *you* sign such a pledge? Give reasons. **C 2.1a, WO 2.1, 2.2**

Key points

- Many people cannot see the problem about couples living together.
- Some regard living together as practice for marriage. Other Christians say that living together spoils the specialness of marriage.

What is abortion?

Abortion is one of the most controversial issues in this book. You must consider all points of view even if you do not agree with them

The law in the UK

Before 1967, abortion was illegal and not openly discussed. If a woman had money, she was discreetly taken to a clinic for an illegal abortion. Her friends would probably think she had had a miscarriage or gone away for a break.

For those without money the only option was 'back street' clinics where untrained people or, occasionally, a retired midwife, performed the abortion. Knitting needles were routinely used for this 'operation', but there was rarely pain relief. Poor hygiene and (sometimes) banned drugs were another feature of back street abortions. Many women **haemorrhaged** and some bled to death rather than go to hospital where their symptoms would be recognized.

Other women tried to do the abortion themselves in hot baths using salt and alcohol. It was not unheard of for women to drown in the bath.

David Steel, a Christian politician, vowed to change the law to end the deaths, injuries and infections endured by women, especially teenagers. Despite bitter opposition the Abortion Act was passed in 1967.

Abortion Act 1967 (revised 1990)

Abortion is legal if two doctors independently agree that one or more of four main reasons for it exist:

- The mother's life is at risk if the pregnancy continues.
- The mother's mental or physical well-being is at risk.
- Scans or tests have shown the baby is badly mentally or physically disabled, or has a deformity meaning it is unlikely to live at birth.

Why do women have abortions?

In some countries such as China, female foetuses are aborted as society only values boys

The mother will die if she continues her pregnancy

The foetus is disabled or deformed (for example, it has spina bifida, has a major heart defect, is deaf and blind, or is unlikely to live when born)

It is used to cover up an affair (questions could be asked which might reveal, for example, that the woman's husband has had a vasectomy)

The mother was raped and became pregnant (every time she sees her baby she will be reminded of her attack and might fear bad traits in the child)

The mother got pregnant by mistake and it is used as a form of contraception

The foetus is carrying a hereditary illness (there are some neurological diseases, only carried by males, in which the sufferer is slowly paralysed; a male foetus would be aborted if the mother agreed)

The mother is underage and would not be able to look after the baby

The mother is underage (sixteen in the UK) and faces physical harm if she goes full term (that is, she is not developed well enough)

- There is a risk of harm to existing children.

The main time limit was lowered from 28 weeks to 24 weeks in 1990. The biological father has no rights and cannot, in law, stop an abortion.

The Roman Catholic view

A Roman Catholic believes that abortion is murder. He or she would quote 'Do not kill' from the Ten Commandments. Roman Catholics believe life begins at conception. In 1968, Pope Paul VI wrote in a Humanae Vitae (a Papal document) that it was an absolute rule for Roman Catholics that abortion was wrong. In 1970, Pope Paul VI reiterated that abortion had always been considered murder since the early church and nothing had changed to alter that view.

The Church of England view

In 1983, the following statement was put forward by the **General Synod** (the government of the Anglican worldwide church):

'The Church of England combines strong opposition to abortion with the recognition that there can be strictly limited conditions under which it may be morally preferable to any alternative.'

The Church believes that the foetus is God-given life and is to 'be nurtured, supported and protected'. The mother is to be shown compassion and her feelings and wishes are to be recognized. The statement continues:

'The foetus has the right to live and develop as a member of the human family; abortion, the termination of life by an act of man, is a great moral evil … It [does not exclude] exceptions, but the right of the innocent to life [means] few exceptions'.

The document concluded that abortions should be carried out early in pregnancy. The numbers of abortions should be cut and more support should be given to pregnant mums.

In the 1997 and 2001 general elections, the Church of England recognized that Christians might want to question candidates on their views on abortion in addition to a range of other moral issues.

The views of other groups

There are other groups who have strong views about abortion.

- *Christians for Free Choice* believe that women should be fully informed about all the options, then allow God to guide them. It says you cannot make one set of rules as all cases are different.

- *SPUC* (Society for the Protection of the Unborn Child) aims to 'defend and promote the existence and value of human life from the moment of conception'. It is also concerned about the welfare of mothers during pregnancy and that of the child. It was the first society in the world to be called **pro-life**. It is non-religious, but most of its members in the UK are Christians, so it is often mistaken for a Christian society.

- *Marie Stopes International* aims to ensure that all people have access to the human right to 'have a child by choice not chance'. It works in over 30 countries, offering contraception, health screening, sterilization, abortion and obstetric care.

- *BPAS* (British Pregnancy Advisory Service) supports women's reproductive choice by providing quality, affordable services for those who wish to prevent pregnancy using contraception or to offer abortion. It also provides sterilization, vasectomy and crisis counselling. It rejects the label pro-abortion. It says it is **pro-choice**.

Views for and against abortion

There are many arguments both for and against abortion. People will be able to justify their reasons and you must accept their views as just as valid as yours.

Arguments for the right to choose

- Every woman has the right to choose, so long as she has information on all the options.
- Women will still have abortions, even if they are illegal. But they would have to rely on back street clinics, which would put them at risk.
- Some Christians say that every child should be wanted. No woman should be forced to carry a child that is not wanted.
- The world population is growing. All couples should have the means to prevent pregnancy so that they can feed their other children and not regard any potential additions as yet 'another mouth to feed'.
- In the case of rape, there are many Christians who would accept abortion on compassionate grounds. They would realize that every time the mother looked at her baby she would remember the horror of it all. If the child was male, she might fear he would have violent traits.
- Some see the foetus as just a collection of cells that cannot survive on their own. So in this case, abortion could be likened to the removal of any unwanted organ.
- If the mother had a life-threatening illness then some would consider abortion justifiable. The mother may already have other children at home. Should they lose their mum and baby?
- Some would question the justification of bringing a disabled baby into the world, especially now there are more and more tests that can determine early on if a child will be disabled. The mother has a choice.
- Many women see it as their **fundamental** right to choose an abortion. They might say that if many men regard it as the woman's duty to

Some would argue that a pregnant mother should be able to make her own choices about her baby.

think about contraception, then she should be able to end the pregnancy if contraception failed.
- There are some Christians who would agree to a male or female foetus being aborted in the cases of certain hereditary diseases, especially some neurological illnesses that strike whole families.

Arguments against abortion

- Many Christians would say that abortion goes against the commandment 'Do not kill'. They believe that the foetus is a new life, so removing it is murder.
- Christians believe that God gives life and only He can take it away.
- Roman Catholics and Christians from other denominations believe that a child is a gift from God. When you make love you should not exclude the possibility of conceiving. So if you do not want a baby, you should not have sex, or you should use a natural way of seeing if the woman is in her fertile time.
- The foetus has rights too, but it cannot voice its opinion.
- There is currently much research about how much pain a foetus can feel. Some medics claim the foetus is in agony as it dies. Some midwives claim the foetus makes unusual movements just before it is aborted. They believe this shows it knows it is about to die.
- Many women suffer post-abortion traumatic stress. Some women will have guilty feelings more than 40 years later.

- Saint Paul reminds Christians that God's **Holy Spirit** lives in our bodies so we must not harm them as God is there.

- Many would say that if a baby is badly disabled then if it is God's will, the mother will miscarry naturally.

Some people would say there is no argument strong enough in support of abortion.

Interview with Jessica

I am pro-choice. I believe that:

- the foetus is a tissue mass and part of the woman

- abortion carries less risk than pregnancy and childbirth

- every child should be wanted; abortion may prevent abuse

- nobody has the right to make me share their moral views

- Jesus never taught about abortion

- every woman has the right to control her own body

- abortion must stay legal, in particular for incest and rape pregnancies

- if abortion is made illegal, back street clinics will open again.

Interview with Jane

I am pro-life. I believe that:

- an unborn foetus is a human being with basic human rights

- a law should be passed giving equal protection to the unborn child

- violence outside abortion clinics is wrong, but I see why they do it

- rape and incest are horrific crimes, which are dealt with in courts of law, but that the unborn child has done no harm

- the NHS wastes resources on abortions

- the Bible supports the view that abortion is murder

- the father should have rights too; this might make some men take a more responsible attitude towards family planning.

Activities

1   Using the Internet, check what the law says about abortion in European countries, such as France, Holland, Denmark, Eire, Russia, China and the USA. Try to display your findings as charts or diagrams. **IT 2.2, 2.3**

2   In the 1997 general election in Britain, and in the 2000 presidential elections in the USA, candidates were asked their views on abortion (often preceding monetary and foreign policy). Do you think this is right? Give reasons for and against this view. **PS 2.1, C 2.1a**

3   Look back at the interviews with Jessica and Jane above and opposite.
    a   Read what each says about rape and incest. Who do you agree with? Why?
    b   Choose two more phrases from each, then say who you agree with and why.
    c   Write your own 'I am pro-choice/life', giving your views on abortion. **PS 1.2**

Key points

- Abortion is controversial. It is one issue that will probably never be resolved.

- Some Christians will never accept abortion because they believe it is murder.

- Others would say that you have to take each case alone as each is unique.

- Some would try to show compassion as Jesus did and also be concerned with quality of life.

Bible passages

Here you will find some Bible passages that can be used for marriage, relationships and abortion (human life). The passages are written out, followed by an explanation. These are by no means the only ones and your teacher may give you other passages to learn.

Mark 10: 2–12

Some Pharisees came and tested [Jesus] by asking, 'Is it lawful for a man to divorce his wife?' 'What did Moses command you?' he replied. They said, 'Moses permitted a man to write a certificate of divorce and send her away.'

'It was because your hearts were hard that Moses wrote you this law,' Jesus replied. 'But at the beginning of creation God "made them male and female". For this reason a man will leave his father and mother and be united to his wife, and the two will become one flesh. So they are no longer two, but one. Therefore what God has joined together, let man not separate.'

When they were in the house again, the disciples asked Jesus about this. He answered, 'Anyone who divorces his wife and marries another woman commits adultery against her. And if she divorces her husband and marries another man, she commits adultery.'

Jesus goes back to the origins of marriage in **Genesis**. The couple leave their families and become one unit. Jesus then says here that there are no circumstances in which divorce is allowed.

This seems to contradict Matthew's and Luke's accounts of what was said. Some scholars suggest that Mark's version is the original teaching of Jesus, but that the early Christians found this too harsh. So when Matthew's and Luke's versions were written or edited they added the words 'except in adultery.'

Matthew 5: 27–32 (Adultery and divorce)

You have heard that it was said, 'Do not commit adultery'. But I tell you that anyone who looks at a woman lustfully has already committed adultery with her in his heart. If your right eye causes you to sin, gouge it out and throw it away. It is better for you to lose one part of your body than for your whole body to be thrown into hell. And if your right hand causes you to sin, cut it off and throw it away. It is better for you to lose one part of your body than for your whole body to go into hell.

It has been said, 'Anyone who divorces his wife must give her a certificate of divorce'. But I tell you that anyone who divorces his wife, except for marital unfaithfulness, causes her to become an adulteress, and anyone who marries the divorced woman commits adultery.

Jesus has been asked a question about remarriage and divorce. He actually adds to the teaching and makes it harder. He makes it clear that divorce is wrong and the only reason for it could be adultery. He then goes on to what is regarded by some as harsh teaching.

Firstly, he says that thinking about sex with another person or lusting after someone in your thoughts is also a sin – you commit adultery in your mind.

Jeremiah 1: 5

Before I formed you in the womb I knew you, before you were born I set you apart; I appointed you as a prophet to the nations.

God has mapped out our lives even before our conception. He has chosen what we will do. So it is not for us to end a new life because God may have great plans for that person. The passage also says that it is not for us to end lives prematurely.

God may still have a job for that person, even if it seems as if there is nothing left for him or her to do.

Psalm 139: 13–16

For you [God] created my inmost being; you knit me together in my mother's womb. I praise you because I am fearfully and wonderfully made; your works are wonderful, I know that full well. My frame was not hidden from you when I was made in the secret place. When I was woven together in the depths of the earth, your eyes saw my unformed body. All the days ordained for me were written in your book before one of them came to be.

This is repeating in poetic form that God maps out our lives and He has decided when we will die, not us. The psalmist is in no doubt that God created the world, continues to create, and each new human is wonderfully made. God has worked out our role in life so we should not prematurely end any life.

Luke 1: 43–4

But why am I so favoured, that the mother of my Lord should come to me? As soon as the sound of your greeting reached my ears, the baby in my womb leaped for joy.

Modern medical science tells us that a baby in the womb can hear well. The baby knows the sound of different voices and will recognize them after birth.

Activities

1 What is the teaching about divorce in the Bible?

2 Mark and Matthew seem to be contradicting Jesus' teaching about divorce. What should Christians do about it if they are considering divorce? How can it be explained?

3 Briefly outline one Bible passage that a Christian could use to support his or her view that abortion is wrong. Then explain what it means. **C 2.2, PS 2.1**

4 If you have access to a concordance, look up abortion. Are there any other good passages you could use? **C 2.2, IT 2.1**

Exam questions to practise

Below are some sample exam questions for paper 2B. To help you score full marks, the first three questions are followed by some tips from examiners. Before attempting the remaining two questions, try to work out your own strategy for approaching them.

1 **a** Explain the term abortion. (2)
   b State two options a Christian might choose instead of having an abortion. (2)

2 Briefly outline one Bible passage that Christians might use to support their belief that divorce is wrong. (2)

3 Explain how the Christian wedding vows help a couple to live their married life. Refer to the vows in your answer. (6)

Now try questions 4 and 5 on your own. Before you write your answers, spend some time thinking of your approach.

4 'Abortion is the greatest evil.' Do you agree? Give reasons for your answer, showing you have thought about more than one point of view. Refer to Christianity in your answer. (5)

5 Explain why the Roman Catholic Church does not allow divorce. (3)

How to score full marks

1 **a** This is a straightforward definition of the word. Do not use the phrase 'the baby is aborted'.
   b The two options must be different. Do not give two types of contraception or two words which mean the same thing.

2 Remember to state who said the words. Make sure you are not quoting from the marriage vows. The commandment 'Do not commit adultery' will not gain any marks if quoted on its own (it says nothing about divorce) unless linked to the question.

3 This is an extended writing essay. One way would be to write out the first vow and explain its meaning and then link it to their married life. You are thinking about life in the future.

Personal issues relating to the sacraments 3

This section includes:

- Holy Orders
- Vocation
- The calling and mission of the laity
- Exam questions to practise.

People are often heard to say phrases like, 'I felt called to work in Peru', or 'I knew early in my life that I would devote myself to God', or 'pay is irrelevant, this is my vocation'. What do they mean? In this section the idea of vocation is discussed. Some choose to take Holy Orders or to lead a religious life in the service of God, whilst others lead lives in the secular world yet still serve God, maybe by using their skills to help those in need by being an active lay member.

Holy Orders

Celibacy An unmarried man or woman who does not have sex.

Elder Early church leader.

Holy Order 'Degree of order'; rank of ordained ministry – bishop, priest and deacon.

Ordain To confer (grant/give) Holy Orders upon someone. Ordination is the ceremony where a person is ordained.

In the Orthodox, Roman Catholic and Anglican churches, there is a rank order of ordained ministry and the main role is priest. In the Orthodox and Roman Catholic churches, **Holy Orders** is one of seven sacraments. The outward, visible sign of the sacrament is the 'laying on of hands' by a bishop or bishops. Sometimes an object associated with the order is given, such as a chalice for a priest. Inwardly, spiritual power and authority are given.

The early church

Acts describes the organization of the early church, for example, Acts 14: 23. Churches were under the leadership of **elders**, although the terms 'elder' and 'bishop' were interchangeable. The first known use of the term 'priest' was in the third century AD. It was applied to bishops as they celebrated the Eucharist. 'Priest' implies a sacrificial role, offering the sacrifice of Jesus in the Mass.

Roman Catholic ordination of a priest

Order of Service

- The candidate is called forward to the bishop.
- The candidate promises to obey the bishop, to celebrate the Eucharist, to preach the Gospel and study and pray to become closer to Christ.
- The candidate lies on the floor, a sign of submitting to God's will and that he needs God's help to do his work. The congregation pray.
- The candidate kneels in front of the bishop who puts his hands on the candidate's head, along with invited priests and bishops. This symbolizes the giving of the Holy Spirit. This part is called the 'laying on of hands'.
- The Consecration Prayer asks God to give him the dignity of priesthood. He is now a priest.
- The bishop anoints him with holy oil on his hands (ready to do God's work). He may be given a chalice and a paten (to hold the wafers of communion).
- The priest is welcomed, then assists the bishop in celebrating High Mass.

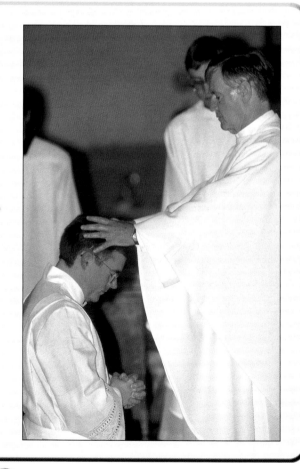

Following the disciples

Roman Catholic bishops believe that they are the successors of the **apostles**. The apostles had so much to do that they delegated to others.

Today, bishops are the heads of dioceses with the task of teaching and leading the church. Bishops **ordain** priests to help them in their care of the church.

The Bishop of Rome is called the Pope and Roman Catholics believe that he is the successor of Peter, the first Bishop of Rome. The Pope is the leader of the bishops, just as Peter appears to have led the disciples.

It is recognized that Order is a sacrament begun by Christ. It is believed that Jesus ordained his disciples at the Last Supper. Priests are distinguished from the laity by the special power of the Holy Spirit. Only men may become priests and they must remain celibate. The argument for and against women priests is on page 68.

Celibacy

In surveys carried out on behalf of the Roman Catholic Church, it was identified that the biggest factor stopping men from becoming priests was the issue of **celibacy**. Many respondents said they would be happy to be unmarried, but could not give up sex. When a man becomes a priest, he accepts a call to be a sacrament of Christ. If you look at a priest, you should see Christ's love, Christ's teaching and his forgiving presence. A priest represents Christ at all times, such as during the Eucharist, when preaching, when absolving sins and when anointing someone who is ill. As such, the priest should be male and celibate.

Many would-be priests worry – can they be happy without a wife, without children? They read about priests who have committed serious sexual offences against children and wonder if celibacy was to blame. They hear tales that celibacy is not natural, that men need sex. One answer would be that all people, whether married or not, are empty until filled with God's power.

What if a man falls in love, can he become a priest? Love is a natural thing, so should it be suppressed? If he falls in love before ordination, he may well be guided into other work (lay member). What would happen if a man is made a priest and then later feels he cannot remain celibate? A man does not become a priest overnight, there is much study and training during which time he can find out if celibacy is right for him. But if he is already a priest, then there is a laid-down procedure for releasing him from his vow of celibacy, but after counselling and retreat.

Anglican priests may marry. Most other denominations now allow women priests/ministers too. Some feel that the Roman Catholic Church is old-fashioned, but Catholics believe that a priest's role model is Christ and as such, male and celibate.

Activities

1   Imagine you are a bishop giving the sermon at an ordination on the role of priesthood. Write out your sermon (between three/five minutes) and then read them out to the rest of the class. Then you can listen to theirs.
    C 2.1a, 2.1b, IT 1.1

2   In groups or on your own:
    a   make a list of opinions for priests being celibate.
    b   make a list of opinions against priests being celibate.
    c   What is your personal opinion? Give reasons. **WO 2.2**

3   In groups, make a list of the qualities you think a potential Roman Catholic priest should have. Which one is the most important? Why? **IT 2.1, WO 2.2**

Vocation

Christ Jesus, who on the shores of the Sea of Galilee called the Apostles and made the foundation of the Church and bearers of your Gospel, in our day, sustain your people on its journey. Give courage to those whom you call to follow you in the priesthood and the consecrated life, so that they may enrich God's field with the wisdom of your word. Make the docile instruments of your love in everyday service of their brothers and sisters.

A prayer for vocations by Pope John Paul II

How can you know a vocation?

A person may know or find out in a variety of ways that they have been called by God to be a priest, to join a religious community, to join a church organization or to go abroad to serve a Christian agency, such as CAFOD.

Some people have the gift of spotting God's calling for others. There are three main questions that can be asked:

1 Desire – Does this person really want this job as a …? Does this person feel excited at the prospect?

2 Motivation – Does Jesus' message in the Gospels motivate this person to share the message of love and service with everyone?

3 Fitness – Does this person know their own gifts/talents, AND their limitations? Does this person trust that God supplies all our needs?

Finding out

Some people think about things for years and then one year they get asked to do something, exactly what they have been thinking about. Some people say they get a dramatic flash/light, or hear a real voice (called Road to Damascus experience, when Paul heard Jesus talking to him alone).

Some people study the Bible and get an inner feeling that the passage(s) have something to say to them. As they read each day, the conviction gets stronger. Other people spend time in prayer and quiet thought and they believe God is speaking to them in their minds. For others, they have never thought about serving God, then the vicar or priest, or someone else says, 'Have you ever thought about …?'

Religious communities

Some Christians feel a calling to live in a religious community. They take vows of poverty, celibacy and obedience. They will devote their lives to working for Christ. Some leave 'worldy, secular' things behind them but work within the world, such as teaching in schools in the UK, or in Mother Teresa schools for poor children in India. Some may be nurses in hospices in the UK or work for CAFOD throughout the world. Others may run hostels for the homeless or run retreat centres.

Others choose to withdraw from the world and live within the walls of their community with little outside contact. They are often self-sufficient or earn money by selling produce like wine and herbal remedies. They will spend the majority of their time worshipping God, praying or contemplating in silence.

Worth Abbey

Prayer is the heart of monastic life

The Abbey church is a symbol of prayer. A monk in Worth Abbey will spend three and a half hours in communal prayer, plus personal prayer and spiritual reading. They believe that if prayer was vital for Jesus, then so it must be for them. The serenity of the abbey creates an atmosphere in which to pray.

Prayer

Prayer was at the heart of Jesus' life, praying before major events in his life-story. For example, before teaching, before beginning his ministry, before healing and throughout his passion. Prayer was his lifeline to God, his Father. Jesus called him 'Abba', which is more like 'dad' than 'father'.

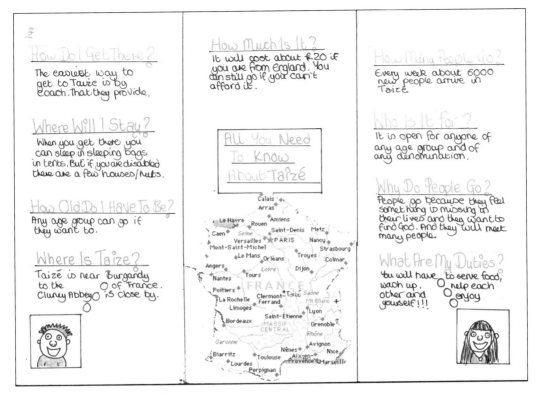

The following is a handwritten student worksheet titled:

All You Need To Know About Taizé

How Do I Get There?
The easiest way to get to Taizé is by coach. That they provide.

Where Will I Stay?
When you get there you can sleep in sleeping bags in tents. But if you are disabled there are a few houses/huts.

How Old Do I Have To Be?
Any age group can go if they want to.

Where Is Taizé?
Taizé is near Burgundy to the O of France. Cluny Abbey O is close by.

How Much Is It?
It will cost about £20 if you are from England. You can still go if your can't afford it.

How Many People Go?
Every week about 6000 new people arrive in Taizé.

Who Is It For?
It is open for anyone of any age group and of any denomination.

Why Do People Go?
People go because they feel something is missing in their lives and they want to find God. And they will meet many people.

What Are My Duties?
You will have to serve food, wash up, help each other and enjoy yourself!!!

Taizé is often studied in schools.

Community and personal prayer

The community of Worth Abbey meets five times a day for prayer together, called The Office. The Office has hymns, psalms, bible readings and prayers. The belief is that each monk becomes a member of the body of Christ as he prays and that the climax of this is the Eucharist, celebrating the death and resurrection of Jesus.

Most monks here spend nearly three hours a day in personal (private) prayer. No guidelines or rules exist, except 'Pray as you can, not as you cannot'.

Taizé

Although of Roman Catholic tradition, Taizé is very much ecumenical. This is a unique community. It is not just for people up to their early twenties, there are family weeks and weeks for married couples. People come from all over the world.
Often 5000 will gather three times a day in church for worship and prayer. Taizé music is recognized world wide, often in Latin, a universal language.

The songs are meditative, made up of short sentences, single words or two line phrases, which are repeated several times. The words express belief and the music takes over the whole person, who becomes receptive to God. Music is regarded as 'heaven's joy on earth'. Sometimes there will be instruments to accompany the singing, often playing a verse without any singing.

Activities

1 Write a paragraph in your own words to explain the term 'vocation'. **PS 2.1**

2 Why do you think many Christians believe you should have a vocation to become a priest or to work for God? **PS 2.1, 2.2**

Key points

- The type of religious life depends on the Order.
- Different people are called to serve God in different ways.

The calling and mission of the laity

Towards the end of the twentieth century, the Roman Catholic Church commissioned several surveys within churches and identified a problem. The majority of **laity** did not understand their role, and over half had never known their role. This was nothing new. A Victorian cartoon said, 'Laity – pay, pray and obey!' Throughout history there has been tension between laity and clergy unsure of the exact role of the laity and how much authority clergy had over laity.

Through baptism Christians are called to a life of service to God helped by the Holy Spirit. Lay people have ministries, gifts and callings to work for God, but not as a priest. Every Christian, clergy or lay, has a responsibility for the mission of the church. Each individual must live the gospel and spread it. There are many callings for laity, including women. In the Roman Catholic and Anglican churches, there is a distinction between laity and clergy, although some might say there is no job description of laity in the Roman Catholic Church.

Different gifts and callings

The call of the clergy is primarily to build up the Church. The call of the laity is primarily to bring the Gospel into the secular world and then bring people to the church, where the clergy would provide the theology if needed.

Laity and worship

This is worship in church. Laity can help in the celebration of the Mass, especially on Sundays, Feast Days and High Days. A person may read from the Bible, lead the prayers, join in the orchestra or singers, carry the cross (crucifer) or play the organ. Some laity are allowed to take communion to the house bound. The Anglican Church has a defined role called 'the Lay Reader', who will undergo three years of practical, theological and academic training.

Their jobs include preaching, handing out bread or wine at communion, leading the service, reading the Bible or leading prayers.

Laity and politics

Laity get involved in politics, for example:

- Campaign for the fair distribution of wealth in the UK.
- Campaign for fair resource distribution in the world.
- Campaign for equality and better resources for the elderly and disabled, locally and further afield.

Laity in their home

Lay people must show Jesus' love in their relationships in everyday life, not just on Sunday. Life with their spouse, children and the extended family are all included and the home should be a place of private and family prayer.

Laity and work

Every Christian must show their beliefs at work, in the way they act, speak, decision-make and their dealings with other people. For example, on the Wirral, Mark, the Christian owner of Mitchell North West Group, which operates a chain of car dealerships, (Lexus, Mitsubishi and Skoda), says they never open on a Sunday, as there is a time for work and a time for play (or re-creation). 'Not all my team are Christians by any means, but each appreciates time away from the business to be with family, friends or neighbours.'

Lay ministry in other denominations

- Methodists have 'lay preachers'. They are allocated to a circuit of about twelve churches. Each circuit has three ordained clergy. Lay preachers serve the remaining nine churches. There is a strict rota so time is equal.
- United Reformed Churches have lay preachers attached to one church.

- Anglicans have lay readers, trained for three years and then licensed in their diocese to preach in that diocese only. They can do everything except celebrate Holy Communion and conduct a church wedding.
- Baptists have lay pastors who are allowed to celebrate Holy Communion. Instead of being paid as a pastor they have a secular job that pays them.

Worth Abbey Lay Community

In 1971, some students asked if they could share the life and prayer of the monastic community. After detailed planning, the students were given a building to turn into their centre. The idea was that people could come to spend time alone in prayer, reflection and service. There would be a core of permanent lay members.

In 2001, the lay community has over 400 members worldwide, young, old, students, the disabled, men, women, single, married, unemployed and from many denominations. There are regular newsletters and members try to visit Worth Abbey as much as possible.

Weekend programme

People who come to use Worth Abbey's facilities share in praying, meditation, reflection and service. Resident lay members always join the monks for four one hour long prayer sessions, silent prayer and the Eucharist once a day. They also study the Bible with the monks. Visitors also help the lay members with practical service, such as cooking and cleaning.

Some of the 400 members live abroad and cannot come regularly, others are parents and cannot get away. Some care for sick relatives. There are many reasons why they cannot visit much or live there, so they live aspects of their life of prayer and service at home. Their main aim is to love God and love their neighbour – this they can do at home. They pray daily, serve others and read the Bible.

There is an annual programme of events, many coinciding with major festivals, for example, carol singing, Easter egg treasure hunt, discussions and celebration and Whitsun outdoor picnics, walks and talks.

Worth Abbey with some of its lay community.

Exam questions to practise

Below are some sample exam questions for paper 2B. To help you score full marks, the first three are followed by some tips from examiners. Before attempting the remaining two questions, try to work out your own strategy for approaching them.

1   Explain the main ways in which those in religious orders contribute to the life of the church. (5)

2   Explain how a lay person can contribute to the life of a parish. (5)

3   Explain why the Roman Catholic Church says that priests must be celibate. (5)

Now try questions 4 and 5 on your own. Before you write your answers, spend some time thinking about your approach.

4   'Monks and nuns find it easy to be Christians, it is the laity in the real world who find the problems!' Do you agree? Give reasons for your answer showing you have thought about more than one point of view. (5)

5   Explain in detail the different role of priests and laity in a parish. (5)

How to score full marks

1   Make a list before you begin, then choose perhaps three or four roles and explain them. Note the key part 'to the life of the church'.

2   Do the same as you did for question **1**. Do not write a long list, choose three of four and write a paragraph on each.

3   This is **not** evaluation so you do not give an opinion. You must explain Roman Catholic teaching and no list writing!

Personal issues relating to the sacraments 4

This section includes:

- Anointing the sick
- Funerals and beliefs about life and death
- What is voluntary euthanasia?
- For and against voluntary euthanasia
- Bible passages
- Exam questions for you to practise.

This section deals with a subject that is often 'taboo', not spoken about and avoided – death and dying. Attitudes to illness and the anointing of the sick are discussed, then funerals and Christian beliefs. Finally voluntary euthanasia is talked about and the positive roles of hospices.

Anointing of the sick

The sacrament of the Anointing of the Sick used to be known as 'Extreme Unction' or the 'Last Rites'. The emphasis of Extreme Unction and the Last Rites was on preparation for dying, preparing for the next life and often used in conjunction with confession and communion.

A new emphasis

The new title of Anointing of the Sick has a new emphasis. It is the pastoral care of the sick. They are anointed with oil as a sign of healing and prayers are said. Cases when this may happen are, for example, before a patient has an operation; for someone who has just been diagnosed with a serious illness; an elderly person; for a baby or child or for someone unwell at home. A person may receive it more than once. Many churches have a special anointing service twice a year during Advent and Lent.

Jesus heals people

All four gospels have many stories about Jesus healing people. In the time of Jesus, people who had epileptic fits or who were mentally ill, were said to have demons in them so Jesus treated them: 'he drove out many demons'. People believed that if you sinned, God punished you by illness. Jesus had compassion for anyone in need. He knew how to deal with different disabilities, for example, he let the blind touch him; he wrote in the sand for the deaf; he held the hand of Jarius' daughter. More importantly, Jesus said a person's faith was vital – you had to believe that you would be healed.

The anointing ceremony

This may take place in a hospital, at home or in church.

- The priest arrives and sprinkles holy water, which calls to mind baptism.

- The priest puts his hands on the patient, then he **anoints** the forehead saying, 'Through this holy anointing, may the Lord … help you.'
- The priest anoints the patient's hands saying, 'May the Lord who frees you from sin, save you and raise you up.'
- The next prayer will be specific to the patient, for example, praying for safety and success in an operation.

Meanings

- The laying on of hands is a sign of welcoming the Holy Spirit, who will give strength and courage.
- The anointing in this context means soothing and healing, your wounds are anointed.
- It is a positive ceremony. The majority of recipients are praying for healing.
- Christians believe that miracles can and do happen, thus they pray on behalf of others.

Effects on a person

- Many patients report feeling a power enter them, to heal them or help them fight and not give in.
- They share in the suffering of Christ and learn more about him. Some report feeling his actual presence.
- Patients may try to start their life afresh.
- Many patients feel more able to cope again. They feel less anxious and many report an inner peace.
- For some, it will be preparation for death. They make amends with God and men.

Interview with Freda

I'm Freda and I'm a 'golden-oldie!' I've just had my 75th birthday and I have so much to thank God for – my family, friends and good health.

I'm finding it difficult at the moment to stay cheerful, as I feel down.

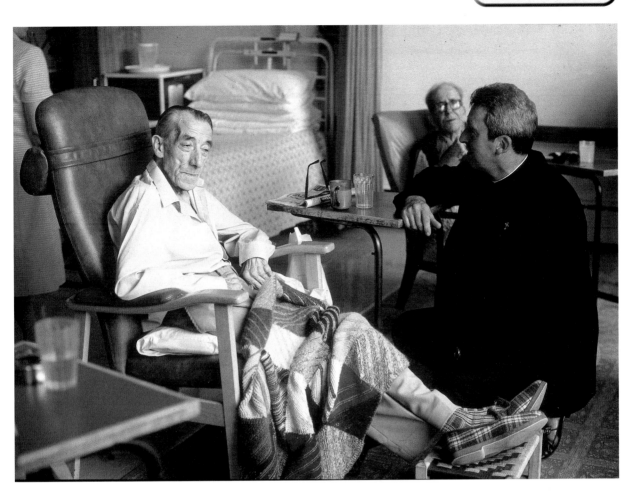

I've been in hospital for a week now – 'Doing tests Freda, you'll soon be right as rain!' They wondered how I would cope with the arthritis pain, well, you do cope, and natural medicines mean healthy living!

One week later

They are sorting out my heart and I will soon be home. But what's changed me is meeting the chaplain, Father David. Bright young thing, gorgeous smile and knew exactly what to say. He held my hand and I said to him that I hadn't been to church in years. 'God still loves you,' he said.

He came the next day and we prayed, well, he did the praying! Then he suggested anointing. I butted in, 'I'm not dying yet!!' He explained that healing was the emphasis now, not death.

He did anoint me and I invited my son and daughter, too. The ceremony was peaceful and full of hope. As Father David prayed, I felt an inner glow, an inner peace. No miracle cure for me, but a cure in my mind! I asked God to have me back. I'm going back to church once I am home. Father David has even persuaded me to compile a book of recipes to sell to raise funds for the scanner appeal.

Activities

1   Do you believe in miracles? Give reasons. Have you heard stories of any miracles? Tell your group. **C 1.1, 2.1a**

2   If you do not believe in miracles, how can they be explained? **PS 2.1, 2.2**

Key points

- Jesus never turned away anyone who needed healing.

- Today, since the Vatican II, the emphasis is on the care of the sick.

Funerals and beliefs about life after death

How it all began

- Jesus was crucified, died and was buried.
- He descended to the dead.
- On the third day, he rose again. This is the **resurrection**.
- He ascended into **heaven** and is seated on the right hand of the Father.
- He will come again to judge the living and the dead.
- Apostles' Creed.

Roman Catholic beliefs

Christians believe in life after death – you leave your earthly body behind and your soul goes to be with God. This is where different Christians disagree. The issue is **purgatory**, a state of preparing for heaven or **hell**. Many Anglicans, Methodists and Baptists (among others) believe that when you die you go straight to heaven or hell, so there is nothing anyone can do once they have died. Groups such as the Roman Catholics teach that the soul goes to purgatory and once prepared, they go to heaven to be with God.

Roman Catholics pray for the souls of the departed. They still need God's mercy and to be forgiven as we are all sinners. The prayer is that the souls may rest in peace. God is a loving and forgiving Father and in time, the souls will enter heaven.

Jesus made it clear that not everyone will go to heaven (see Matthew 7: 21). Judgement is also based on how people respond to those in need, such as the parable of the sheep and the goats in Matthew 25: 31–46.

What is heaven like?

Unfortunately, no human has been to heaven and back to give a description. The Bible does give some clues, often in imagery and picture form.

- Luke 14: 15–24. Jesus describes heaven as a banquet and great feast.
- Luke 23: 24. Jesus promises that the penitent thief will go to paradise and be with God.
- Paul wrote a lot on the subject and 1 Corinthians: 15 has much detail.
  - Verses 3–11. Paul lists eye witnesses who met Jesus, in the form of an early **creed**.
  - Verses 12–19, 29–32. Paul says that if Jesus did not come to life again, then all their beliefs and teaching are false. Martyred Christians would have died for nothing and Paul would be a fake.
  - Verse 18. Paul describes death as 'falling asleep'.
  - Verses 35–49. Paul says that when you die you leave behind your physical body, 'it is dust', and you are given a spiritual body and will look like Jesus, 'we bear the likeness of the man from heaven.'
  - Verses 54–8. Paul says that Jesus has victory over sin and death. Verses 55–7 is one of the earliest hymns quoted. Death should no longer be feared as the end. For many, it is just the start, a new beginning.

When Princess Diana died, the whole nation showed it's grief.

A Roman Catholic funeral service

Any Christian funeral service includes a celebration of the life of the dead person. There will be sadness and often much grief, but the undertone should always be one of hope and trust in God.

The order of service

Most Roman Catholics will request a requiem Mass and to pray for the soul of the departed.

- The coffin is sprinkled with holy water, bringing to mind the baptism of the departed.
- A Bible, a book of gospels, or a cross is placed on the coffin as a symbol of Christian life. The gospels guided the departed.
- Liturgy of the Word – suitable Bible readings, prayers and at least one tribute/short sermon.
- Liturgy of the Eucharist.
- Final prayers for relatives and then the person's soul is committed to God.
- A song of farewell is sung as the priest sprinkles the coffin with holy water and uses incense.

The coffin will be taken to be buried or cremated. Usually only close relatives or friends go for the Committal. The words 'Dust to dust, ashes to ashes' are spoken and if buried, loved ones throw handfuls of earth on to the coffin.

Suitable readings

John 3: 16 says, 'God so loved the world that he gave his Son, so that whoever believes in him should not perish, instead will have eternal life.'

Romans 8: 38 and 39 says, 'Neither death, nor angels, nor powers, nor kingdoms, nor things past, present or future will be able to separate Christians from God's love for us.'

1 Corinthians 2: 9 reminds us that 'No eye has seen, no ear has heard ... what God has prepared for those who love and believe in him.'

Flowers

At the end of the nineteenth century, a coffin would usually be smothered in mounds of flowers. By the end of the twentieth century, the general trend has moved away from this. Families tend to suggest that flowers be done by arrangement and that a donation to a favoured charity would be preferable.

Many people who leave a will state their chosen charities. Often far more money is raised than would have bought flowers, which die and are of no use. Money can be used to bring new life.

A new tradition began with the Hillsborough disaster. People placed bunches of flowers where it happened and at Anfield on the pitches, along with scarves and hats. Bunches of flowers now appear at the site of a fatal accident (for example, tied to a fence) or where a murder victim was found.

The biggest mass out-pouring of sorrow was at the death of Princess Diana in 1997. People openly cried, millions of bunches of flowers were placed at strategic points and a new air of solidarity was shown. Millions of pounds were raised for charities, such as specialist cancer nurses for children.

Activities

1 In groups, make a list of the role of priests and laity in helping a bereaved family. **WO 1.2**

2 Why do you think proper counselling is important? Give reasons. **C 1.1, 2.1**

3 Which charity would you choose to put in your will? Why? **C 1.1, 2.1**

Key points

- For many people death is taboo and something not to be talked about.
- Christians believe in a life after death.
- The role of the church is to offer prayer and support.

What is voluntary euthanasia?

Voluntary euthanasia is a controversial issue with Christians supporting both sides of the argument. With voluntary euthanasia the patient – and no one else – makes the decision. The patient may ask someone – often a doctor or relative – to help him or her to die. The person must be in a sound mental state and able to make a lucid decision. If the relatives make the decision for the patient or the patient is in a coma, then this is not voluntary euthanasia.

Other names for voluntary euthanasia

Voluntary euthanasia is known by a variety of names including **assisted suicide**, **mercy killing** and gentle, easy death. As the law stands in the UK, anyone who helps the patient to die is called an accessory to murder. Some insurance companies may regard it as **suicide** but others may not if the person was dying anyway.

- *Assisted suicide* means someone helps the patient to die. Supporters of voluntary euthanasia do not agree that it is suicide. They prefer to think of it as a form of 'putting to sleep'.

  Suicide is different. It is killing oneself. The reasons for this could include failure in exams or a relationship. Suicide is sometimes a cry for help. The person does not really want to die but needs attention.

- *Mercy killing* means helping a terminally ill person to die so he or she can be free of pain. It is showing compassion (mercy). The patient –

who could be dying of **AIDS** or cancer – requests to die and the person asked takes pity on them and agrees to help. Death is often by lethal injection. It can be compared to putting sick animals to sleep.

- *Gentle, easy death* means helping someone to die quickly in dignity. Supporters distinguish this from suicide because the person is already dying or suffering pain. The patient wants to die in peace, often requesting to die in his or her own home, in his or her own bed, with his or her family around. He does not want to die alone.

Members of Exit can apply for a book on methods of dying.

In the Netherlands, patients have the right to ask a doctor to be allowed to die and their request will be considered.

Living will

This is when a patient declares in advance that they do not wish to be kept alive by a machine.

What churches say

Different churches give different advice on the subject of voluntary euthanasia. Different Christians have their own beliefs, too.

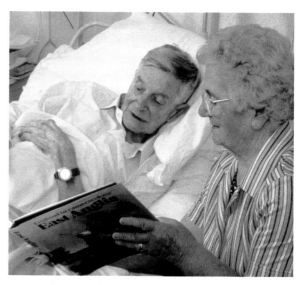

Terminally ill people often want peace and dignity in the way they die.

- *Roman Catholic* guidance states euthanasia is wrong. Life is sacred. Only God can make decisions over death. Different Popes have said that euthanasia contributed to a 'profound change in the way life and relationships between people are considered'. It is considered a 'grave violation of the Law of God'. Cardinal Basil Hume said in April 1995 that he was '200 per cent behind the Pope's plea that society should stop and ask where all this could lead'. Roman Catholics do accept that it is right to ease the suffering of those terminally ill, often knowing that the side effects of powerful drugs may well speed up the death of the patient. This is considered natural, because it is a side effect.

- The Synod, on behalf of the *Church of England* reiterates the rights of humans to be valued. Those who are ill become vulnerable and need special care. In 1993, the Synod published a report that said no change in the law was needed. In other words, a person has a right to refuse treatment, but he or she does not have the right in law to die at a time of his choosing. The Synod also saw a difference between letting a person die by, for example, not giving them antibiotics and deliberate killing by overdose.

    Exit has published the results of several opinion polls which claim that many Christians, up to 23 per cent, agree that doctors should be allowed to help an incurably ill patient to die if they so wish.

What other groups say

- Exit advocates a change in the law to allow the judiciary greater flexibility concerning euthanasia. It studies the law on various cases and closely examines statements by politicians. It also advises on living wills so they are acceptable and legal in a court of law.

Exit: promoting euthanasia and advising on legal acceptability.

Activities

1 Why do you think voluntary euthanasia is still illegal in the UK? Discuss as a whole class or in groups (groups need to share their ideas). A good place to help you make up your mind is with the Exit website (www.euthanasia.org). **C 2.1a, IT 2.1**

2 Why do you think people of all persuasions are watching the Netherlands closely since voluntary euthanasia was legalized? Give reasons. **PS 2.1, C 2.1a**

3 Do you think groups like Exit should publish information about how to take your life in dignity? Give reasons. **C 2.1a, PS 2.1**

Key points

- Voluntary euthanasia is when the patient decides he or she wants to die because he or she is going to die soon in any case, or is in great pain.

- Voluntary euthanasia is controversial.

- People on both sides watch events in the Netherlands carefully, where euthanasia is legalized, to see the effects on attitudes.

For and against voluntary euthanasia

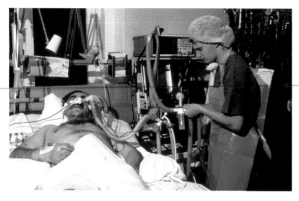

Should people have the right to request that they want to die?

There are arguments for and against voluntary euthanasia. People are able to justify their points of view, and you must accept their view as just as valid as yours.

Arguments for voluntary euthanasia

- If a person has the right to eat or drink what he or she likes, smoke, pierce his or her body and do things to excess, then he or she also has the right to decide when to die, if his or her suffering gets too much.

- Some Christians believe that total healing will be in heaven, so all they are doing is speeding things up. Many people pray for healing and do not realize that healing may not be on earth.

- Why should suffering be prolonged? It is terrible for the patient and for their families and friends. Some family members find it so hard to accept the suffering that they feel they can no longer visit the patient, or they get so emotional that everyone ends up in tears.

- The patient wants to die with dignity and believes he or she has that right. The patient may fear loss of control over bodily functions and having to have literally everything done for him or her.

- The patient wants to die in his or her own bed at home, with other family members there at the time of death.

- Some Christians say that the Bible does not state that a person must be kept alive at any cost. They would also say that Jesus always showed compassion and voluntary euthanasia is just that. In Jesus' day, if people became ill there was relatively little that could be done to keep them alive. The question of prolonging life with antibiotics was not an issue. Therefore he did not teach directly about it.

Against voluntary euthanasia

- God gives life, so only He can decide when to take it away. Life is a precious gift. Ending that life should not be our decision. It goes against the commandment 'Do not kill'. Killing the patient is not an accident. It is a deliberate action.

- The patient might not really be in a fit state to make a logical decision, despite promises of safeguards, such as psychological tests to ensure his or her brain is not muddled by drugs. The patient might change his or her mind on a day when he or she feels better.

- Doctors promise to save life. Voluntary euthanasia may be showing mercy, but it is not saving life.

- The doctor may be proved wrong – a miracle may take place or the treatment might work. Many Christians believe in miracles and they pray for the healing of the friend.

- Helping the sick teaches compassion and patience to the carers. Christians believe that nursing the sick is one way of helping Jesus. He was often portrayed healing all kinds of diseases and many of his parables mention people helping those in need – such as the good Samaritan.

- Some Christians believe that suffering is a way of strengthening faith and trust in God. They would say it is part of life and not for us to question. It is God's plan for them – this is a more extreme view but held by some.

- Christians believe that people's moral conscience will change. Gradually people will accept it as normal. Once medics begin killing, the guilt will fade away. Once society accepts it, where will it lead? For example, will all babies born with certain conditions be allowed to die? There is also the example of Manchester GP Harold Shipman, who killed once and could not stop. He claimed he helped his first victim to die on her request and he 'liked' killing. He was jailed in 2000 for fifteen murders. After police investigations, it is thought he may have killed another 192 patients.

Hospices

The first recorded hospices were founded in the Middle Ages by Christian knights, such as Knights Templar, who cared for those badly injured in the **Crusades**. Monks and nuns also looked after the sick in the Abbeys. They grew herbs and flowers in the monastery gardens to make into medicines and potions. Recently, modern historians have made up these potions, medicines and ointments and found many to be very effective. Some of the principles of **homeopathy** were experimented with by the monks.

In the twentieth century, Dame Cicely Saunders, a Christian doctor, helped to found the modern hospice movement.

Terminally ill people who are dying of illnesses, such as AIDS and cancer, are cared for in hospices until they die. Hospices also provide **respite care** so that carers also get a break.

The patients are cared for by a wide range of trained staff, such as doctors, nurses, physiotherapists, aromatherapists, speech therapists, counsellors and pain relief specialists.

Fears about death are discussed with the patient and their relatives and friends. they can talk to a specially trained counsellor or therapist, or they may choose to speak to a chaplain.

Hospices are often at the forefront of pain relief research and research into terminal illness. Many patients offer to take part in trials of new drugs and therapies. Many people find inner peace and tranquility before they die. Whatever your Christian allegiance or religion, nobody is turned away, nor is the ability to pay or make a big donation an issue.

Activities

1 Read the poem below.

I have to make the journey alone
I'd like to make it now.
I'd like to gently slip away if only I knew
    how.
I cannot bear the helpless stare, I'm
    ready to let go of the hand.
If I asked for my heart to stop its beat,
    would they ever understand?
'All in God's time,' is what they'd say,
    'you may go into remission
We hate it too – what you're going
    through but we cannot give
    permission.'
Can they not see the indignity, the
    dependence that fills me with
    shame?
Would it be such a sin to release my
    soul from its helpless tortured
    frame?

a What is stopping the person from killing him or herself?
b Why do 'they' (those in the medical profession and the family) disagree with the wish to die?
c List two reasons given by the patient why death is an option. **PS 2.1, 2.2**
2 Write a poem about voluntary euthanasia. (You can work in pairs.) It can be for or against, or it can put forward both views. All the poems can be read out loud to the class. **C 2.3, WO 2.2, 2.3**

Key points

- One of the main arguments supporting voluntary euthanasia is that we should show compassion and respect the patient's wishes.
- Against voluntary euthanasia is the worry about where it will lead to. If you can legally kill, society's moral conscience may change.

Here you will find some relevant Bible passages. The passages are written out, then there is an explanation of what they mean.

James 5: 13–16 (Sickness and healing)

Is any one of you in trouble? He should pray. Is anyone happy? Let him sing songs of praise. Is any one of you sick? He should call the elders of the church to pray over him and anoint him with oil in the name of the Lord.

And the prayer offered in faith will make the sick person well; the Lord will raise him up. If he has sinned, he will be forgiven.

Therefore confess your sins to each other and pray for each other so that you may be healed. The prayer of a righteous man is powerful and effective.

Jesus is giving advice to the early Christians. One rule of the elders in each church was to pray for sick members. They also could anoint the sick with holy oil. James suggests that real, physical healing can take place. He also stresses the power of prayer by other people. He too likens healing with forgiveness of sin.

1 Corinthians 6: 18–20 (Body as a temple)

Flee from sexual immorality. All other sins a man commits are outside his body, but he who sins sexually sins against his own body. Do you not know that your body is a temple of the Holy Spirit, who is in you, whom you have received from God? You are not your own; you were bought at a price. Therefore honour God with your body.

Paul says we must be careful what we do with and to our bodies, as God lives in our bodies. He is present as the Holy Spirit. Those against abortion may say killing the foetus harms the body. Not only does it kill a new life within the woman, but it can also damage her. No abortion is without risk.

Voluntary euthanasia is actually killing your human body regardless of your beliefs about life after death. If you ask someone to help you it is still harming your body.

Jeremiah 1: 5

Before I formed you in the womb I knew you, before you were born I set you apart; I appointed you as a prophet to the nations.

God has mapped out our lives even before our conception. He has chosen what we will do. So it is not for us to end a new life, because God may have great plans for that person. The passage also says that it is not for us to end lives prematurely. God may still have a job for that person, even if it seems as if there is nothing left for him or her to do.

Psalm 139: 13–16

For you [God] created my inmost being; you knit me together in my mother's womb. I praise you because I am fearfully and wonderfully made; your works are wonderful, I know that full well. My frame was not hidden from you when I was made in the secret place. When I was woven together in the depths of the earth, your eyes saw my unformed body. All the days ordained for me were written in your book before one of them came to be.

This is repeating in poetic form that God maps out our lives and He has decided when we will die, not us. The psalmist is in no doubt that God created the world, continues to create and each new human is wonderfully made. God has worked out our role in life so we should not prematurely end any life.

Luke 12: 4–7

Do not be afraid of those who kill the body and after that can do no more. But I will show you whom you should fear: Fear him who, after the killing of the body, has power to throw you into hell. Yes, I tell you, fear him. Are not five sparrows sold for two pennies? Yet not one of them is forgotten by God. Indeed, the very hairs of your head are all numbered. Don't be afraid; you are worth more than many sparrows.

Jesus gets across the point that God cares for us. We should respect God, who will judge our lives. If He cares for sparrows then He surely treats us as more precious. Opponents of abortion would say that God cares and children are a gift of God. He also cares for those who suffer. However, others say Jesus did not teach specifically about abortion or voluntary euthanasia.

In conclusion

There is a link between the different sacraments. If taken seriously, each sacrament will have an effect on people's lives. It is no use giving the Peace to people in the congregation during Mass if you are in the middle of an argument at home. It is no use getting confirmed and making promises, then never going to church. Some Christians say that babies should not be baptized unless the parent(s) are regular church attenders.

People serve God in different ways and feel called in many ways. We cannot all be 'Mother Teresas', or other well-known Christians, but we can all serve God in some way, whether at home, work, or in a Christian organization (like the Salvation Army or in a developing or war torn country supported by CAFOD). Most of us will get little or no recognition, but we do it for God.

Abortion and euthanasia are probably the most contentious issues – their link is 'How do we value human life?' What are our feelings about disability? A badly disabled foetus can be 'disposed of', but we cannot go into the future to see if predictions were right. A terminally ill patient may feel that no one wants a disabled person who needs constant care and so should they offer to die or should the doctors decide?

In the end, most issues are left to individuals to make up their own minds. Some say, 'I will think about it if the need arises for me.' The Bible tells us that we were created by him and he has mapped out our lives. Trusting God to supply our needs and the ability to cope are lessons to learn.

A real miracle

June 1998

Sam kept on complaining about pains in his left leg. 'Growing pains of a fifteen-year-old.' Then the PE teacher noticed that Sam walked crab-like and had a red patch. Hospital, tests, bad news. He had a tumour in his leg that had got to the bone. The only solution was amputation. His mother, Jackie, went to see the hospital chaplain. She marched in and said, 'Reverend! I have never been to church and Sam isn't baptized. But if there is a God, then cure him!'

Reverend David came to see Sam as the operation was due the following afternoon. Sam lay quietly as David prayed and then touched his leg. Sam felt a hotness, the nurse saw a glow and his mother, in the parents room, felt a jolt. Sam sat up and felt an inner peace.

The next morning, Sam noticed that the red patch was gone and he could walk properly. They did a final scan of his leg. There was a shock. Did they have the right notes? There wasn't a trace of the tumour!

His mother is now a church member, as is Sam who is training to be a physiotherapist.

Activities

1 Briefly outline one Bible passage that a Christian could use to support his or her view that voluntary euthanasia is wrong. Then explain what it means. **C 2.2, PS 2.1**

2 Some Christians believe that God can even have work for the terminally ill person to do. Try and list some things this person could do. You could work in groups. **WO 2.2, 2.3**

3 Do you believe in miracles? **PS 2.1, 2.2**

4 Do you think the Bible is right to imply that illness is caused by sin? **PS 2.1, 2.2**

Exam questions to practise

Below are some sample questions for paper 2B. To help you score full marks, the first three questions are followed by some tips from examiners. Before attempting the remaining questions, try to work out your own strategy for approaching them.

1 **a** What advice does James give in his letter about caring for the sick? (3)
   b What can be learned about mercy and forgiveness from the parable of the unmerciful servant? (3)

2 Outline the main features of a Roman Catholic funeral. Explain how it reflects what Roman Catholics believe about life after death. In your answer you may refer to:
   a preparations for the service,
   b the service of Requiem Mass,
   c the burial or cremation. (8)

3 Explain two different Christian attitudes towards voluntary euthanasia. (8)

Now try questions 4 and 5 on your own. Before you write your answers, spend some time thinking about your approach.

4 Explain what part the Sacrament of Anointing the Sick might play in the life of a Roman Catholic. In your answer, you should refer to:
   a the purpose of this sacrament.
   b Roman Catholic beliefs about the effects of this sacrament. (8)

5 'Money spent on funerals is a waste. It could be put to much better use.' Do you agree? Give reasons for your answer, showing that you have thought about more than one point of view. You should refer to Christianity in your answer. (6)

How to score full marks

1 **a** Do not write out the passage, but pick out the relevant points.
   b Again, do not write out the parable. Select the meaning.

2 The key is 'Explain how it reflects what Roman Catholics believe about life after death'. Concentrate on this part of the funeral.

3 4 marks are given to each view, so you can write plenty and explain it clearly.

Coursework

For this GCSE you will have to produce one piece of coursework of 1,000 to 1,500 words on 'The effects of the Roman Catholic tradition upon aspects of Christian lifestyle and behaviour'. You will be assessed on the following.

- What you know about moral issues from a Christian perspective and how it has affected what people believe and do. (Knowledge.)
- Your ability to explain what Christians believe and how their beliefs affect the way they live and worship. (Understanding.)
- Your ability to give a personal opinion and to show other points of view. (Evaluation.)

You will be marked separately on each of these three objectives.
It is important that all three skills are shown.

Knowledge

The aim here is not to write down as much information as you can! You need to show that you have selected the information that is answering the question.

Understanding

This part is to show that you understand the information you are writing down. So, for example, if the task is to 'Choose two problems that people in developing countries face and explain how agencies can help solve the problems', you need to explain how Christians might apply their beliefs about helping the poor to solve these problems.

You must show you understand:
- key words and their meaning – for example, 'vocation'
- religious importance – for example, 'When you help someone in need you are helping Jesus himself'
- people's feelings and emotions – for example, showing humility.

Evaluation

This is giving your opinion, what you think. But you must also show you understand more than one point of view. You do not have to give a personal judgement. Instead you could give one view for and one view against the given quote.

Writing your assignment

Make sure you understand what you have to do. Read the title a number of times and try to see what the assignment is really about.

Books

- Make sure you only use books that you understand.
- Keep to the point.
- Do not copy large chunks – stick to short quotations.
- If you quote from another source, put it in inverted commas.
- In the bibliography and coursework cover sheet you must note all books used – title, author and publisher.

Internet

- There is no extra credit for using the Internet.
- Make sure you do not copy large chunks from the Internet – you must select your own, short quotes.
- Websites are sometimes full of irrelevant information, so be aware of this.
- In the bibliography and cover sheet you must write down the full website address (for example, www. …) and the title of the article.

Interviews

- Decide carefully who you want to interview and why (for example, a soldier who has seen active service).

- Decide beforehand exactly what questions you will ask.

- Before you begin the interview, explain why you are doing it and let the person you are interviewing know questions you are going to ask.

- If you want to use a tape to record the interview, then ask first.

- Evaluation is important – what is this person's opinion?

Surveys

These can be useful, but you must go prepared.

- What are you trying to find out? Prepare the questions.

- How will you record responses? Ticks? Writing down an answer?

- Decide how many people you wish to interview and where. Do you need permission first? For example, if you interview people going to church, you should tell the vicar first.

- How will you present your findings? A graph, for example?

Your coursework

- If you are unsure about anything, before you write things down and while you are doing it, ASK YOUR TEACHER.

- Check spelling, punctuation and grammar. If you use a computer to do this, set it to UK spellings (not American).

- If the question tells you, for example, to use a Bible passage, you will lose marks if you do not.

- If a page goes wrong, then start again!

- Begin each part of the question on a separate piece of paper. Some choose only to use single-sided, but that is up to you.

- Only number the pages once you have finished, in case you need to add something.

- Try and use the correct religious terms – for example, Jesus taught using parables. Do not write, 'Jesus taught using stories'.

Finished!

- Read the finished assignment at least twice. Check that you have answered all parts of the question.

- Remember to check you have noted down all books, websites and so on that you have used.

- Count the number of words – there are no extra marks if you go over.

Glossary

Abortion The deliberate termination (ending) of a pregnancy, usually before 24 weeks, for a variety of issues, such as severe disability of the foetus

Absolution Being freed of a sin, pardoned by a priest

Adultery Sex between a married man and a woman not his wife and/or a married woman and a man not her husband. Sometimes called 'an affair'

Aid Help sent to countries in need, either in an emergency or over the long term

AIDS Acquired Immune Deficiency Syndrome. This is the destruction of the body's immune system, resulting from a virus called HIV. Being HIV positive does not mean you will get AIDS, but it does mean the immune system has no defence. The virus is passed between people through body fluids, mainly blood and semen. It is often passed on by having sex without a condom or by drug users sharing needles. It cannot be caught by touching

Aim of punishment The reason for the choice of punishment, thinking about the expected result/outcome

ANC (African National Congress) The main opposition group in South Africa. It opposed apartheid using violence. Led by Nelson Mandela

Annulment The Roman Catholic Church does not recognize divorce. They can offer annulment, which effectively cancels out the marriage as if it never took place. There are various reasons why people seek annulments – for example, one partner was forced into the marriage, or because sex between the partners never took place

Anoint To apply oil, in this case, Holy Oil

Apartheid Official policy in South Africa of segregating black and white people. This usually worked to the disadvantage of the black population

Apostle Greek, meaning 'a sent one'. Jesus chose twelve special followers. They became apostles, sent into the world. These apostles set up the early church, were authority figures and attributed much to New Testament teaching

Assisted suicide An alternative name for voluntary euthanasia. A patient is helped to die by someone else at the patient's request

Baptism The act of Christian initiation joining by sprinkling, pouring or immersing in water

Beatitude From the Latin meaning 'blessedness'

Believers' (adult) baptism A person makes up his or her own mind to be baptized, understanding the commitment and making his/her own promises. The Baptist Church fully immerses in baptism

Boycott (South Africa) To refuse to deal with. In this context many countries refused to trade with South Africa or to buy their produce. Sporting teams and athletes were banned from international events

Boycott (USA) The most famous boycott in the USA was the Bus Boycott. Black people refused to take the buses until they were treated the same as white people

Capital punishment Punishment by death, the criminal is executed

CARE and Education (Christian Action Research Campaign) This organization aims to protect the family unit, children and the elderly. It also aims to be vocal and petition Parliament

Catechism Christians are taught these beliefs by the use of questions and answers

Catholic 'Universal' or 'worldwide'. 'One holy, catholic church' means the church is universal, not restricted to one country or one race of people

Celebrant The priest who celebrates the mass

Celibacy Choosing to remain unmarried and not have sex. Roman Catholic priests vow to be celibate

Chastity Not having sex until marriage. In Medieval times it also meant no sex for the wife while her husband went on a Crusade

Civil war War between citizens of the same country/state

Civilian A person who is not military – for example, not a soldier

Commandment Something you must do or obey

Commitment A pledge or undertaking lasting the rest of one's life

Communicant The person who receives communion

Confirmation The completion of baptism, the person 'confirms' their beliefs for himself/herself

Conscientious objector Person who objects to a specific war on the grounds of conscience. The person may feel there is no just cause for the war

Consummated A marriage has been completed by having sex

Creeds Come from the Latin 'credo' (I believe). These are summary statements of Christian beliefs, originally used to instruct new converts, then incorporated into worship

Crime Breaking the law of the land – for example, speeding

Crusades Military expeditions under the banner of the Cross to recover the Holy Land from the Turks

Death Row Section of prison where those sentenced to death are kept. The cells are laid out in long rows

Debt Money that is owed. In this context, the money is owed by one country to another

Denomination A group of churches (and congregations) with the same theological beliefs – for example, Anglicans, Roman Catholics and Baptists

Developing country Used to be called a third world country. It is a poor country commonly in parts of Africa, South America, Asia and India. It does not have much, if any, technology and is often in debt to Western banks

Disarmament Getting rid of weapons. Sometimes it refers to terrorist groups giving up of all their weapons

Disciple One who is a disciplined learner and an adherent to the teachings/beliefs of their teacher

Discrimination Prejudice in action. It is acting differently towards someone (or a group) due to, for example, gender, race or age. It may take many forms, such as not giving someone a job, bullying, fighting or name calling

Disease Illness that may cause early death, disfigurement or disability

Divorce The legal ending of a marriage by a law court

Elder Early church leader

Evangelical churches Churches of all denominations which focus on telling non-Christians the Good News. They often work in poverty-stricken areas of the UK and are seen as outgoing and lively

Fidelity Being faithful, in this context to your husband or wife

Fornication Sexual activity outside marriage. Sex before marriage

Fundamental 'Basic'. In this context it refers to Christians who wish to get back to the basics of Christianity, such as the Virgin Birth and the Resurrection

G8 countries USA, Canada, Japan, UK, Germany, France, Italy and Russia. They meet annually to discuss world issues. In 2000, a key issue was debt relief for poor countries

General Synod The ruling body of the Anglican Church in England made up of elected bishops and clergy and elected lay people

Genesis 'Beginnings.' The Book of Genesis describes the origins of the world and the roots of religion and the Jewish race

Gift Aid A taxpayer gives a lump sum to a charity. (The Chancellor varies the maximum amount per year in the Budget.) The charity can then reclaim the tax paid from the Inland Revenue

Godparent A male or female sponsor at baptism

Gospels Books attributed to Matthew, Mark, Luke and John, telling the life story of Jesus

Habitat Natural home of an animal, plant, insect and so on

Haemorrhage Very heavy bleeding, which is often life-threatening

Heaven Being with God

Hell Separation from God

Holy Communion Also called the Mass, the Eucharist, the Lord's Supper or the Last Supper, depending on the denomination. It remembers Jesus' last meal with his apostles when he said the bread and the wine would symbolize his body and blood on the cross

Holy Order 'Degree of order'; rank of ordained ministry – bishop, priest and deacon

Holy Spirit God sends Christians the Holy Spirit to guide and inspire them, the power within them. Also described as 'God around us'

Holy War War fought in the belief that God is on their side

Homeopathy Treatment of an illness by small doses of natural elements/drugs that would produce symptoms of the illness in a healthy person who has not got that illness

Homosexual Men who have a sexual attraction for other men

Hospice A home for the care of the terminally ill. Often run as a charity relying on donations; many are Christian run jointly by several denominations

Immersion To put right under water

Jingoism Excessive patriotism

Just war War that a Christian believes has a right cause. It is an attempt to justify war. There are five basic criteria against which the war is set

Kingdom of God The reign of God as King over creation. Jesus proclaimed the news of this kingdom and taught in parables. In a sense, the kingdom has arrived now, but at the same time Christians wait for Christ's second coming

Laity People who are not clergy, not ordained

Lepers People who were made total outcasts because they had a skin disease which was thought to be highly contagious. They lived with other lepers in colonies. They were not allowed to go near other people. Food was left for them, rather than handed to them

Liturgy A prescribed form of public worship, the ritual. For example Anglicans, Roman Catholics and the Orthodox follow set patterns of worship for the service of Holy Communion

Living will A person's advance declaration to enable him or her to refuse unwanted life-prolonging treatment before a time when he is not able to say it for himself or herself – for example, the person is in a coma but does not wish to be put on life support or given antibiotics

Long-term aid Aid spread over many years with the goal of self-reliance to those receiving it. One important part is providing education to communities

Lutheran Church Church founded by Martin Luther, the famous German protestant reformer (1483–1546). Not to be confused with Martin Luther King of the USA (1929–68)

Malnutrition Not having a balanced, regular diet, vital nutrients are missing. It leads to illnesses, but the World Health Organization recognizes it as an illness in itself

Marriage Being married, joined as husband and wife

Martyrs People who die or are prepared to die for their beliefs, often religious

Mass Also called Holy Communion, the Eucharist or the Lord's Supper. This ceremony remembers Jesus' last meal with his disciples. He instructed them to 'do this in my memory'

Media Television, radio, newspapers – in other words, those who communicate with the public

Mercy killing Another term for voluntary euthanasia. It occurs when someone takes compassion on the patient's request to die and agrees to help that person die with dignity

Myth A story often with imaginary people, objects and animals – for example, a unicorn. Myths often try to explain the unexplainable, such as creation. They explain why something happened, rather than how

Nationalism Often one step on from being patriotic. A person wants his or her country united, sometimes with the removal of some groups/races of people. In the twenty-first century it also means a country fighting for independence

NATO (North Atlantic Treaty Organization) It now has nineteen full member countries, the aim of which is to help each other's defence. NATO works on security structures for Europe. NATO troops are used to keep the peace in countries such as Kosovo, in the former Yugoslavia

Nicene Creed A statement of Christian beliefs in summary form, agreed at the Council of Nicaea in AD 325

Non-violent protest Peaceful protest. The protesters set out to demonstrate in peace using tactics like sit-ins or boycotts. Sometimes they are met by violence from those sent to break up the protest

NSPCC (National Society for the Prevention of Cruelty to Children) Founded in the nineteenth century it aims to end child abuse. It is still in business at the forefront of work against all types of child abuse and cruelty

Nuclear weapons Weapons of mass destruction, causing radioactive explosion and contamination

Ordain To confer (grant/give) Holy Orders upon someone Ordination is the ceremony where a person is ordained

Orthodox Church Church which split from the Roman Catholic Church. Now mainly found in Eastern Europe, for example, the Russian Orthodox Church

Pacifist A person who believes that all wars and all fighting are wrong

Poverty cycle People who are poor cannot afford an education so have unskilled jobs. These are often low-paid, and so the cycle develops and continues. It is difficult to get out of this poverty trap

Prejudice Prejudging, having a biased thought or attitude about a person or group because of race or religion, for example

Primary health care The aim is to prevent disease (easier to prevent than cure). Schemes include clean water provision, midwife training and teaching about nutrition

Pro-choice A person who believes that the woman has the right to choose to have an abortion or not, based on the knowledge of the alternatives

Pro-life A person who believes the foetus is a living human being, with full rights to a life. Abortion is murder as life begins at conception

Purgatory Preparation for heaven or hell

Reconciliation To restore friendship. In a Christian context can also mean being brought back to God

Refugees People who flee from an area often with only what they can carry, and then cross an international border (into another country), escaping religious, racial or political persecution. If the person stays in the same country, he or she is often referred to as 'displaced'

Remarriage Getting married again but to a different partner. This can happen after the death of a spouse, or after divorce or annulment

Repentance (penitence) To be sorry for wrong doing and to try and put things right

Respite care An adult or child who is ill or disabled who needs constant care and who is looked after at home by family is taken to a special home/hospice/hospital or even someone else's home, to give the carers a break or a holiday. Sometimes a respite carer comes to the house on a regular basis to allow the carer to, for example, leave the house and do some shopping

Resistance A secret opposition group in World War II, opposing Nazi occupation. Particularly active in France, among other activities they carried out sabotage and rescued RAF pilots who had crashed

Resurrection Rising up, here meaning Jesus coming back to life again

Righteous A morally good person

Sacrament 'Visible form of an invisible grace.' It is a sign of a sacred thing, a religious ceremony or ritual through which you come to know God better. The two main sacraments, recognized by most denominations, are Baptism and Holy Communion. These are the ones begun by Jesus. Roman Catholics also have confirmation, penance, marriage, ordination and Extreme Unction (Last Rites)

Segregation A split or separation from others

Sexism Discrimination based on gender

Shanty town An area of a city, often on the worst land, where housing is makeshift, made out of anything the occupant can find. Often a breeding ground for disease due to the lack of sanitation and running water

Short-term aid Emergency aid sent due to a disaster, such as a hurricane or flood. Aid includes tents, food and medical provisions

Sin Breaking God's law in thought, the spoken word or what you do – for example, stealing

Social Services A department in all local councils providing help and care for the elderly, children, the disabled and the sick

SS, The The chief paramilitary force in Nazi Germany. It began as Hitler's bodyguard and expanded to become the Nazi party militia and internal police force. It controlled the Gestapo, the police and the concentration camps

Suicide The act of killing yourself, often while mentally unstable

Tenakh The Jewish scriptures

Terrorist People who use the threat of violence to create a climate of fear to bring about change or to get their own way in a political situation

Testimony Evidence. In this case, a person who is to be baptized briefly tells how they came to this decision

Theology The systematic (methodical) study of religion and religious beliefs

United Nations (UN) Countries of the world meet together and discuss world issues. One of their first documents was the Declaration of Human Rights

Vaccination To protect against disease by injecting with a vaccine – for example, measles vaccine to prevent measles

Vocation A calling to a particular job or career, in this context, a calling by God

Voluntary euthanasia If a patient is dying and in great pain, he or she may prefer to choose to die. He may also ask someone to help him die. If the person is in a coma and on life support, and relatives decide to switch off that support, it is known as 'involuntary'

Vows Solemn promises

War Armed conflict between two or more opposing groups

Weapons of mass destruction Nuclear and chemical weapons that are indiscriminate and kill thousands of people in one go, or where the effects can last for years. Examples include radioactive contamination of the land, and babies born with deformities

Wedding The actual marriage ceremony

Youth Offending Teams (YOTs) These were set up in every local authority with the aim of identifying young people who commit crime or who are likely to, and to help prevent crime. Various agencies are co-ordinated by the YOT in the hope that action will happen quickly

Index